Feb. 5, 202[illegible]

To [illegible]

Fr[illegible]

[illegible]

suffer a [illegible] you

op
"kunch" delivered

by the HART.

my soul and spirit

need pampering:

~~ppppppppp~~

**There is properly no history,
only biography.
—*Ralph Waldo Emerson***

* * * * * * * * * * * * * * * * *

The Making of America series traces the constitutional history of the United States through overlapping biographies of American men and women. The debates that raged when our nation was founded have been argued ever since: *How should the Constitution be interpreted? What is the meaning, and where are the limits, of personal liberty? What is the proper role of the federal government? Who should be included in "we the people"?* Each biography in the series tells the story of an American leader who helped shape the United States of today.

THURGOOD MARSHALL

The Making of America

★ TERI KANEFIELD ★

Abrams Books for Young Readers
New York

TO MY FAMILY

The following images are courtesy of Alamy: Page vi, 30,000 Protestors. Page 11, Thurgood Marshall, age 2. Page 185, LBJ and Thurgood Marshall. Page 215, House of Representatives, 1939. The following images are courtesy of Getty: Page 2, Women Protestors. Page 129, bus in front of Tar Paper School. Page 200, Ruth Bader Ginsburg. Pages 216–217, House of Representatives, 2018. The following images are courtesy of the *Afro-American*: Page 12, Thurgood's parents. Page 113, Irene Morgan. Page 117, Spottswood Robinson and Oliver Hill. Courtesy of Lincoln University: Page 78, Lloyd Gaines. Courtesy of Spelman College: Page 128, Barbara Johns. Page 221: Fred Schilling, Collection of the Supreme Court of the United States. All other images are public domain, courtesy of the National Archives, Baltimore Archives, the Smithsonian, or the Library of Congress.

Cataloging-in-Publication Data has been applied for
and may be obtained from the Library of Congress.

ISBN 978-1-4197-4104-3

Text copyright © 2020 Teri Kanefield
Edited by Howard W. Reeves
Book design by Sara Corbett

Abrams Books for Young Readers are available at special discounts when purchased in quantity for premiums and promotions as well as fundraising or educational use. Special editions can also be created to specification. For details, contact specialsales@abramsbooks.com or the address below.

Abrams® and The Making of America® are
registered trademarks of Harry N. Abrams, Inc.

ABRAMS The Art of Books
195 Broadway, New York, NY 10007
abramsbooks.com

CONTENTS

A Public Enemy

The year was 1967. America was in tumult. African Americans were protesting in the streets, demanding equality. Women, too, were demanding equality, and they, too, were marching. A few militants even talked about using violence to secure equal rights for African Americans. People were protesting the war in Vietnam. Some of the protesters openly flouted the law. College campuses and cities

Thirty thousand Civil Rights demonstrators gathered outside the Alabama State capitol following their march from Selma to Montgomery, 1965.

A crowd protesting in front of the Capitol, 1967. Pictured in the center is Stokely Carmichael, a civil rights leader of the 1960s.

1969: A women's liberation march. The women are marching for both women's liberation and black equality.

like San Francisco were hotbeds of what was called counter-culture unrest, with young people rejecting what they thought of as restrictive traditional values. They rejected the idea that African Americans were expected to be content with second-class citizenship. They rejected the notion that women should limit their career ambitions to jobs deemed appropriate, like secretary, nurse, or elementary school teacher.

It seemed to many that America was unraveling. Large swaths of the population, mostly in southern, suburban, and rural communities, were alarmed and angry about these upheavals. Many of them placed the blame on one man: Thurgood Marshall.

Thurgood Marshall was the lawyer who had dedicated his career to ending racial segregation. His work culminated in a 1954 Supreme Court decision called *Brown v. Board of Education*, the case that outlawed racial segregation in schools. *Brown v. Board of Education* disrupted the South and became a catalyst for the civil rights movement, which in turn paved the way for the women's rights movement and the 1960s counterculture revolution.

In the words of one U.S. senator, Thurgood Marshall "was considered a public enemy of the South."

✹ ✹ ✹ ✹ ✹ ✹ ✹ ✹ ✹ ✹ ✹ ✹ ✹ ✹ ✹

O n June 13, 1967, President Lyndon B. Johnson—who hailed from Texas and had long been an advocate of racial equality under the law—called a press conference. He stood in the White House Rose Garden next to Thurgood Marshall and announced that he was nominating Marshall to the United States Supreme Court.

"I believe he has already earned his place in history," President Johnson told the assembled crowd, "but I think it will be greatly enhanced by his service on the Court. I believe he earned that appointment . . . he is the best qualified by training and by very valuable service to the country."

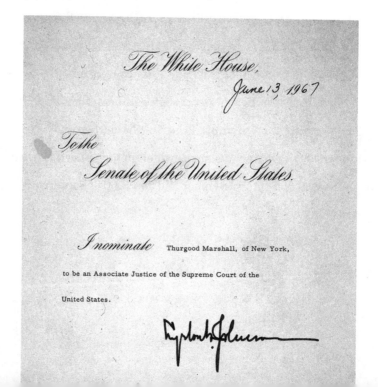

The White House,
June 13, 1967

To the
Senate of the United States.

I nominate Thurgood Marshall, of New York,

to be an Associate Justice of the Supreme Court of the

United States.

Lyndon B. Johnson

The word spread like a wildfire. Letters poured in to the president and members of Congress. Some people were thrilled. Others were horrified. "Please, sir, no N— on the Supreme Court bench," came a typical letter, "with looting and burning and riots all over the country . . . so many feel as we do."

Senator Strom Thurmond from South Carolina was determined to block Marshall's nomination. He was the author of the *Southern Manifesto*, a 1956 document denouncing efforts by the federal government to end segregation. Thurmond joined with three other southern senators: John McClellan from Arkansas, Sam Ervin from North Carolina, and James Eastland of Mississippi. All four were on the Senate Judiciary Committee, so they would have a chance to question Thurgood Marshall in an open hearing. All four resented what Thurgood Marshall had done in their states as an activist lawyer.

Senator Thurmond told his staff to start digging. He wanted dirt he could use to prevent Marshall from taking a place on the United States Supreme Court. His research team plunged into their task. Hearings would begin within a few weeks. They didn't have much time to come up with a plan.

President Johnson nominates Thurgood Marshall to be an associate Supreme Court Justice.

1

Way Up South

*"It was taken for granted that we had to make
something of ourselves. Not much was said about it;
it was just in the atmosphere of the home."*

—Thurgood Marshall

hurgood Marshall loved telling stories. He particularly
enjoyed telling about his great-great-grandfather on
his mother's side, a notorious rebel whom Thurgood
proudly proclaimed was the "baddest N— in the whole
state of Maryland." As one version of the story went,
his master captured him in Africa and brought him to work at
his Eastern Shore plantation. According to family legend, he was
from Sierra Leone. "But we all know," Thurgood liked to say,
"that he really came from the toughest part of the Congo."

One day—as Thurgood liked to tell the story—the exasperated master said, "Now, look—you are so ornery and mean to white people that you'll never be a good servant, and I in good conscience can't sell you to another white person." So his master offered him a deal: "If you agree to leave the county and the state, I'll turn you loose and give you your freedom."

"I'm not going anyplace," said the ornery slave. His master gave him his freedom anyway. He married a white woman and settled down as a free man on a farm not far from his old master. Eventually his descendants made their way to Baltimore. "I'm proud of a guy like that," Thurgood said.

✳ ✳ ✳ ✳ ✳ ✳ ✳ ✳ ✳ ✳ ✳ ✳ ✳ ✳ ✳

Baltimore, in the nineteenth and early twentieth centuries, was an exceptional place. In the North, there were so few African Americans that integration was impossible. Further south, the very idea of integration was so repugnant that white southerners fought tooth and nail to prevent it. Throughout the nation, African Americans largely remained in poverty and cut off from opportunities available to whites. Baltimore was different. Maryland was situated just south of the Mason-Dixon line—between the North and South—and had the largest free

African American population in the nation. In the part of the city known as Old West Baltimore, whites and African Americans lived in close proximity, and the two races interacted daily. Many African Americans thrived. They became well-to-do homeowners and successful business owners. There were even top-notch private schools for African American children. Later Thurgood Marshall referred to Baltimore as "way up South."

Thurgood Marshall's maternal grandmother, Mary Fossett, was a twelve-year-old free African American girl in Baltimore at the start of the Civil War. She was able to read chilling newspaper accounts of the fighting. She later became a schoolteacher.

Only one of Thurgood Marshall's grandparents was enslaved when the Civil War broke out—the grandfather for whom he was named: Thoroughgood Marshall. Thoroughgood escaped slavery during the chaos that ensued when the Confederates fired on Fort Sumter. He went to Baltimore and blended in with the free African Americans. His race was listed in public records as "mulatto." He went by the nickname Thorney Good, which he thought suited him better than Thoroughgood.

In Baltimore, Thorney Good worked as a waiter. Later he joined the army and went to Texas with the all-black Twenty-Fourth Regiment of the U.S. Cavalry. After being discharged in

1874, he returned to Baltimore and married a neighbor, Annie Robinson. Their first child, William Marshall, was Thurgood's father.

Thorney Good and Annie opened the T. G. Marshall store on the corner of Dolphin and Division Streets, both bustling thoroughfares. They sold groceries and dry goods. It became one of the most prosperous stores in Old West Baltimore. Thorney Good and Annie thrived.

Thorney Good Marshall standing in front of the T. G. Marshall Grocery. This image originally appeared in a souvenir booklet for a black business convention in Baltimore in March 1908.

One day the electric company came to install a power pole on the sidewalk directly in front of the store. Annie was having none of it. She marched outside and told the workmen it was *her* sidewalk and she didn't want a pole in the middle of it. She shooed them away. They returned with a court order allowing them to install a pole. Annie came outside with her kitchen chair, and placed it over the designated spot on the sidewalk. In the chair she sat. She refused to budge. "This went on for days and weeks," Thurgood said, "and finally Grandma Annie emerged as the victor of what may have been the first successful sit-down strike in Maryland."

Thurgood Marshall's maternal grandparents, Isaiah Olive Branch Williams and Mary Fossett Williams, also owned a successful Baltimore store. Their store was located near a well-to-do white neighborhood. Not far away, low-income African Americans lived in a crowded alley. "The door was left open to the basement of his home and store," Thurgood Marshall later explained, "and the poor Negroes that lived in back had access to go down there and get wood, coal, and vegetables and stuff. And he would tell them, 'Now, don't take more than you need.' Nobody ever did."

★ ★ ★ ★ ★ ★ ★ ★ ★ ★ ★ ★ ★ ★

Thurgood—whose real name was Thoroughgood—was born on July 2, 1908 in Old West Baltimore. The neighborhood into which he was born was a vibrant, thriving community consisting of about sixty city blocks of row houses, grocery stores, tailor shops, movie houses, barber shops, pharmacies, with a doctor's office on almost every block. Many of Thoroughgood's aunts and uncles, as well as all four grandparents, were politically active and prominent members of the community.

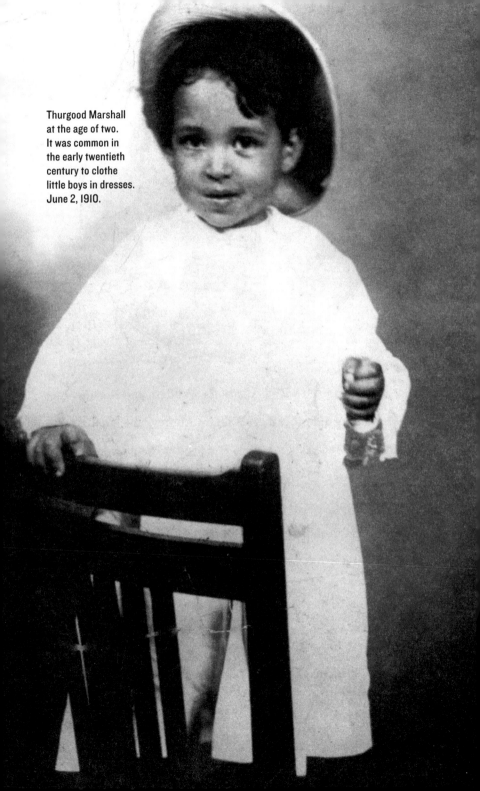

Thurgood Marshall at the age of two. It was common in the early twentieth century to clothe little boys in dresses. June 2, 1910.

William and
Norma Marshall,
undated

Thurgood lived with his parents, William and Norma Marshall, and his older brother, William Aubrey, in a small apartment at 53 McChechen Street. His brother went by his middle name, Aubrey. Thurgood was two years old when his family moved to Harlem. His father hoped to find work on one of the New York railroads, or as a waiter in one of New York's prestigious establishments. The Marshalls lived with his mother's sister and brother-in-law, Denmedia and Clarence, who went by the nicknames Medi and Boots. William found work as a waiter for the New York Central Railroad.

Harlem at that time was rapidly becoming known as a cultural center where African American writers, religious leaders, and musicians gathered to debate politics and the future of the African American race. Thurgood's father's friends included both blacks and whites. He wasn't afraid to stand up to white people. He told his sons to respect all people, but never tolerate disrespect. "If somebody calls you a N—," he said, "take it up right then and there. Either win or lose right then and there." When William Marshall wanted to compliment someone, he said, "That's very black of you." When white people mentioned his light skin, he told them that his mother was white and his father was African American. It wasn't true, but he "got a bang out of shocking white people." At the time there were strict laws against the races marrying, and many whites became enraged at the mere idea of an African American man marrying a white woman.

Thurgood's mother, Norma, played piano, enjoyed reading, and was somewhat prim. She had more formal schooling than her husband, and was very strong-minded. She was active in several women's clubs that raised money for the local branch of the NAACP (pronounced *N double-A C P*)—the National Association for the Advancement of Colored People, an organization formed in 1909 to work for equal rights for African Americans. "My father was the noisiest and loudest," Thurgood later said, "but my mother was by far the strongest."

Thurgood brought home strays. The first time he came home with a stray—a smelly half-starved gray cat—his mother told him to "get that cat out of here." He pleaded until she let him give the cat a saucer of milk. Eventually his mother started giving in when he showed up with animals or people in need of care. "Our home got to be known as the 'Friendly Inn,'" she explained later.

If someone said or did something Thurgood thought was wrong, he fought back. When a neighbor slapped his head, he responded with fury. He frequently argued with his father. He and his brother, Aubrey, had opposite personalities: Thurgood was the talker and debater; Aubrey, who was more introverted, liked science. The brothers were very young when they decided on their respective professions: Aubrey would be a doctor, Thurgood a lawyer.

When Thurgood was six years old, his family moved back to Old West Baltimore so Norma could care for her ailing mother. They moved in with one of Thurgood's paternal uncles. Russian, German, and Italian immigrants lived in West Baltimore, but the neighborhood was still predominantly African American.

"In the department stores downtown," Thurgood said, "a Negro was not allowed to buy anything off the counters. As you went into the store, you were told to get the h— out." When African Americans *were* permitted into stores, they were not allowed to try clothes on. If they wanted to purchase shoes, they drew the outlines of their feet and the clerks determined their sizes. When African Americans made purchases, their receipts were marked "final sale." Nothing could be returned or exchanged. Also humiliating was having to go to the back door of a restaurant to purchase a sandwich if the restaurant didn't permit African Americans inside.

For Thurgood, the worst was that "There were no toilet facilities available to Negros in the downtown area, and I remember one day, I had to go, and the only thing I could do was get on a trolley car and try to get home." Once he didn't make it in time.

Laws that enforced racial segregation were called Jim Crow laws. "Jump Jim Crow" was the name of a minstrel routine performed in 1828 by white men wearing blackface. The term came to be derogatory for African Americans and thus descriptive of their lives segregated from whites. Jim Crow laws included laws requiring African Americans to attend separate schools, sit in certain railway cars, drink from separate drinking fountains, and other restrictions.

WAITING ROOM
FOR WHITES
ONLY
BY ORDER OF
POLICE DEPT.

During the Jim Crow era, signs like this one were common.

★ ★ ★ ★ ★ ★ ★ ★ ★ ★ ★ ★ ★ ★ ★

The schools were strictly segregated. Thurgood attended Henry Highland Garnett School 103, which served children from kindergarten through eighth grade. There was no play area at School 103, so when school was in session, the road in front of the school was closed and used as a recreation and sports area. The teachers lived in the neighborhood. Parents and teachers teamed up to make sure the youngsters studied and took school seriously. Norma kept a close eye on her sons' homework and grades.

Children playing in front of School 103, Baltimore

One family friend described Thurgood as "a jolly boy who always had something to say." She also recalled seeing him "coming down Division Street every Sunday afternoon around one o'clock. He'd be wearing knee pants with both hands dug way into his pockets and be kicking a stone in front of him as he crossed over to Dolphin Street to visit his grandparents at their big grocery store on the corner . . . He was in a deep study, that boy, and it was plain something was going on inside of him."

Thurgood was in second grade when he announced that his name, Thoroughgood, was too long and just too much. He told his family he wished to be called "Thurgood," a nickname he invented. From then on, he was Thurgood Marshall.

Thurgood got his first paying job in a neighborhood store when he was seven. Customers were allowed to call in their orders. Thurgood's job was to pick out their items and deliver them in his red wagon. He earned a small wage and all he could eat.

"In Baltimore, where I was brought up," Thurgood explained later, "we lived on a respectable street, but behind us there were back alleys where the roughnecks and the tough kids hung out. When it was time for dinner, my mother used to go to the front door and call my older brother. Then she'd go to the back door and call me."

Hanging out in the streets and alleys toughened Thurgood. Black and white children played together. Thurgood and his classmates, though, didn't get along with the boys in the all-white Catholic elementary school located a few blocks from his school. "They were practically all Italians, and we used to have periodic fights—not too bad. Maybe a rock here and there. It was fists, and eventually they let them out [of school] fifteen minutes before we got out so that they could get home." Many years later, when Thurgood was practicing law, an assistant state's attorney approached him. Thurgood didn't recognize him. "Well, if you don't remember me, I remember you," the man said to Thurgood. He pointed to a small scar on his forehead. That jogged Thurgood's memory: He'd thrown the rock that had left the scar.

Thurgood's best friend was a Jewish boy named Sammy Hale. Thurgood was annoyed when Sammy let people call him "kike" without fighting back. ("Kike" was a derogatory word for Jews.) "If anybody called me a 'N—,' I fought 'em," Thurgood said.

As Thurgood grew older, his arguments with his father, William Marshall, became more heated. "We had the most violent arguments you ever heard about anything," Thurgood said later. "I guess we argued five out of seven nights at the dinner table." They argued about current events, world problems, race relations, and even the law. Sometimes their debates would continue for days. During the breaks, Thurgood thought over his position and refined his arguments. He later credited his father with preparing him for a legal career. "He did it by teaching me to argue, by challenging my logic on every point, by making me prove every statement. He never told me to be a lawyer, but he turned me into one."

Thurgood Marshall
in high school

Thurgood, along with a number of other gifted students, skipped a grade, so, a year early, he and the others entered the Colored High and Training School (now known as Frederick Douglass High School). That was the year his parents were finally able to afford their own house. They bought a house on Druid Hill Avenue. The mortgage payment created financial hardship, particularly because Norma and William wanted to save for college for both boys. Norma was working as a schoolteacher. William's salary paid the mortgage and expenses; her salary went into a savings account for college tuition. Thurgood and Aubrey always had after-school jobs to help out.

Thurgood, who was always large for his age, grew to be six feet two inches tall. Because he was so tall and lanky, his nickname was Legs. His favorite teacher was Gough Decatur McDaniels, who taught history. Mr. McDaniels encouraged Thurgood to join the debate team. Thurgood did, and he thrived. He was elected captain of the freshman team. "He could outtalk and out-argue anybody," said one of his classmates. Thurgood developed a wonderful speaking voice: deep and melodious.

Thurgood's seat in one classroom was by a window, giving him a view of a Baltimore police station. He watched as suspects, mostly African American, were brought in by officers on the all-white police force. Thurgood knew from stories in the neighborhood that African American suspects who were questioned about crimes were often hit with a club or brass knuckles to get them to talk. Thurgood later explained that when the classroom windows were open, he could hear police officers beating people, saying, "Black boy, why don't you just shut your mouth, you're going to talk yourself into the electric chair." One of Thurgood's classmates later recalled that Thurgood was so riveted by what was happening at the police station that the teacher had to tell him to close the blinds.

Thurgood's father noticed that Thurgood was keenly aware of the injustices African Americans suffered. William Marshall kept up with current events and even followed pending court cases. Sometimes when he had a free afternoon, he went to court to listen to the proceedings. He began taking Thurgood to court with him to watch.

Thurgood himself was arrested and saw the inside of the police station when he was fifteen. He was working as a delivery boy for a family-owned clothing store, delivering hats and items of clothing to customers, a job that required him to ride the trollies around Baltimore. One day, the five o'clock rush hour was in full swing when he tried to board a crowded trolley. He was carrying five hats in a large box. He felt someone grab him by the collar and pull him off the trolley. The guy who had grabbed him, a white man, said, "Don't push in front of a white lady."

"D— it," Thurgood said, "I'm just trying to get on the d— bus."

The man glared at him and said, "N—, don't you talk to me like that."

Thurgood dropped the hats and started swinging at the man. The man trampled the hats and tried to wrestle Thurgood to the ground, but Thurgood kept throwing punches. A crowd gathered. People on the trolley gawked. A policeman ran over and pushed into the fray. The officer didn't say a word to the white man. Without asking any questions, he arrested Thurgood and took him to the station. From there, Thurgood called his employer, Mr. Schoen.

Mr. Schoen hurried to the police station. Thurgood apologized to Mr. Schoen for the damage to the hats. "Forget about them," Mr. Schoen said. "What about you?" Thurgood told him what had happened. Mr. Schoen called his lawyer, who talked the officers into letting Thurgood go without charging him.

As Thurgood and Mr. Schoen walked home, Mr. Schoen asked, "Did the man really call you N—?"

"Yes, sir," Thurgood said, "he sure did."

Mr. Schoen stopped walking, put his arm on Thurgood's shoulder, and told him he had done the right thing. Later, when Thurgood became an advocate for racial equality, he retold the story to make a point about the decency of whites like Mr. Schoen.

The incident, combined with widespread stories of lynchings, had a deep and lasting effect on Thurgood.

Lynchings were mob killings. An angry mob of whites would accuse an African American of committing a crime. The mob would then declare him guilty, sentence him to death, and kill him on the spot. Often the crimes of which African Americans were accused were not actually crimes. African Americans were lynched for being "uppity" and not paying enough respect to whites. Black men were often lynched after being accused of improprieties with white women.

After that incident on the bus, Thurgood was afraid to be around white women, terrified that sudden violence would erupt should he get too close. "I never felt good around them," he said.

Years later, when he was in college and traveling with the debate team, he was seated next to a white woman at a celebratory dinner at Harvard. He recalled feeling intensely uncomfortable. "But I managed to just grin and bear it," he said.

★ ★ ★ ★ ★ ★ ★ ★ ★ ★ ★ ★ ★ ★ ★

In school, Thurgood earned a reputation as a rowdy prankster. Once, when the teacher left the room, he threw a piece of chalk that hit a classmate in the eye. "He didn't aim to hit me in the eye," she said later. "He just threw the chalk. He was mischievous that way." Thurgood said that when he acted up in high school, the principal sent him to the basement with a copy of the Constitution and told him to memorize part of it. "Before I left that school," Thurgood said, "I knew the whole thing by heart."

The Thirteenth, Fourteenth, and Fifteenth Amendments, enacted after the Civil War, ended slavery and were intended to make African Americans equal citizens of the United States. The Thirteenth Amendment outlawed slavery. The Fourteenth Amendment, among other things, guaranteed all citizens equal protection of the laws. The

He was puzzled to read the part of the Fourteenth Amendment that guarantees "equal protection of the laws" to all citizens. Anyone could look around and see that African Americans did not enjoy equal protection of the laws. He asked his father about it. William Marshall told him that the Constitution described things as they should be, not as they were.

Thurgood wanted to go to Lincoln University, a university known as the Princeton for African Americans because of its reputation for academic excellence and because so many professors were Princeton graduates. His high school grades were good enough for admission. The problem was paying the tuition. During Thurgood's last year of high school, his father fell ill and couldn't work. Aubrey was already a student at Lincoln, and Norma was having trouble making both the mortgage and the tuition payments.

Fifteenth Amendment allowed African American men to vote. Women—black and white—could not vote until the passage of the Nineteenth Amendment in 1920. It wasn't long, though, before communities, particularly in the South, began passing laws depriving African Americans of their rights, including legislation making it difficult to vote.

Thurgood finished up his classwork a semester early so that he could work full time to help save the tuition money. He found a job as a waiter on a dining car for the B&O Railroad. The white waiters were unionized, but the African Americans were forbidden to form or join unions. They earned much less than whites, and they were not given overtime pay. One day, an African American waiter was talking to a few others, including Thurgood, about the need for an African American union. Not long after the train arrived in Baltimore, the white inspector of dining cars boarded and went directly to the waiter who had led the discussion. He tapped him on the shoulder and said, "Get your clothes. You're fired." Nobody knew how the inspector had found out about the discussion so quickly. After that, Thurgood was careful to keep quiet. He needed the job.

Thurgood graduated from high school on June 24, 1925. With his first year of tuition money saved, he was able to enter Lincoln University in the fall.

Thurgood's mother wanted Thurgood to become a dentist because she believed dentistry was a good profession for African Americans. There was a high demand for African American dentists. White dentists generally didn't give African American patients the same quality of care. If an African American patient had a toothache, for example, the dentist simply pulled the tooth instead of trying to save it.

Thurgood—bowing to pressure from his mother—sometimes said he wanted to become a dentist. He added later that he couldn't because he had trouble with science. When he filled out his college application, however, he answered the question "What do you plan as your life's work?" by writing: "A lawyer."

② College Days

"None of us got where we are solely by pulling ourselves up by our bootstraps. We got here because somebody—a parent, a teacher, an Ivy League crony or a few nuns—bent down and helped us pick up our boots."

—Thurgood Marshall

incoln University, surrounded by open fields and woods, was located about four miles from Oxford, Pennsylvania. When Thurgood arrived in the fall of 1925, about three hundred students were enrolled. The school was all male. The students were mostly African American, with a few whites from the local community. The poet Langston Hughes was in Thurgood's first-year class. Hughes, who was six years older, had already achieved national renown for his book of poems called *The Negro Speaks of Rivers*.

College Days

Thurgood threw himself into campus social life. He didn't spend much time studying. He said, "I just eased along—you know, do good enough to pass." He played a lot of pinochle, read comic books, attended sporting events, became a fan of cowboy movies, and worked in the campus bakery. With his buddies, he made frequent trips to Philadelphia, hoping to meet young women. His brother, Aubrey, was a senior, but Aubrey and Thurgood moved in different circles. Aubrey was more serious and studious. Thurgood enjoyed parties and a good laugh.

Thurgood's favorite class was modern history. He tried out for the debate team and performed so well that he became the first freshman in the history of the university to win a spot on the varsity debate team. He enjoyed everything about being on the team: researching the topics, practicing his arguments, and traveling to various competitions.

Rendall Hall, Lincoln University, Pennsylvania, 1930

Whenever Thurgood and Aubrey returned home for a visit, the neighbor, Mrs. Hall, would say to her husband, "Ah, the boys are home." She always knew they were back because she heard Thurgood and William's raucous dinner table arguments through the walls.

The Marshall family's financial situation improved when William recovered his health and went back to work as the head steward at the Gibson Island Club on Chesapeake Bay, a club for wealthy Baltimore whites. He was in charge of hiring and managing the African American staff.

At the end of Thurgood's first year of college, William hired Thurgood as a summer waiter. Thurgood became one of the most popular waiters. One day, a prominent U.S. senator saw Thurgood and shouted, "Hey, N—, I want service at this table." Not wanting to lose his job, Thurgood did as he was ordered. When the dinner was over, the senator left a whopping twenty-dollar tip. (Twenty dollars was equivalent to almost two weeks' salary for Thurgood.)

The following evening, the senator came back and again spoke to Thurgood rudely. Thurgood leaped to do whatever the senator ordered. The senator left another twenty-dollar tip. This happened evening after evening. It was the easiest money Thurgood had ever earned. One night his father overheard the senator call his son a "N—." He watched, enraged, as his son responded by meekly doing whatever the senator demanded. He pulled Thurgood aside and said, "You're fired! You are a disgrace to the colored people!" Thurgood told his father about the twenty-dollar tips. William, stunned, agreed that it was worth twenty dollars to be called a N—. Thurgood joked with his father that "the minute [he] runs out of them twenties, I'm going to bust [him] in the nose."

During Thurgood's second year of college, he participated in the first-ever debate between an African American college and a white college when Lincoln University faced off against Pennsylvania State University. The topic was the Eighteenth Amendment, outlawing alcohol (which was later repealed). The question was whether the amendment should be modified to permit the manufacture and sale of light wines and beer. The judges deliberated a long time and then voted two to one for Penn State.

During Thurgood's third year of college, the Lincoln team debated New York's City College, National Students' Union of England, and others, each time to thunderous applause. Also, during his third year, Lincoln debated the Liberal Club of Harvard University on the topic of whether "further intermixing of races in the United States is desirable." The topic drew the ire of the local chapter of the Ku Klux Klan (KKK), who demanded that the topic be changed.

The Ku Klux Klan was founded in the South after the Civil War. Klan members were unabashed white supremacists and violently opposed civil rights for African Americans. They were also against any mixing of the races. Klan members intimidated African Americans into accepting second-class citizenship. They wore white hooded costumes, went on night rides and committed such atrocities as tarring and feathering and murder.

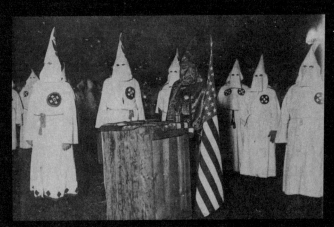

Klan members often went on what they called "night rides" to terrify African Americans.

College Days

When the organizers of the debate at Harvard refused to change the topic, Klan members threw rocks and broke the windows of the Liberal Club's building. The Klan, however, was unable to stop the debate, which drew an audience of two thousand. Neither side was declared the winner, so both sides were honored equally at a celebratory dinner at Harvard that evening. Thurgood and his teammates stayed the night in one of Harvard's dormitories, where they were treated like honored guests. This also enraged the Ku Klux Klan.

✷ ✷ ✷ ✷ ✷ ✷ ✷ ✷ ✷ ✷ ✷ ✷ ✷ ✷ ✷

One day Thurgood was talking to a fellow student who was from a place that was not segregated. Later, when Thurgood recounted the story, he couldn't remember where his classmate was from. As they talked, Thurgood told him all the things an African American person couldn't do in Baltimore. His fellow student asked, "How do you know it?"

"Everybody knows it," Thurgood said.

"Well, did you ever try?"

Thurgood, of course, had never tried. Later he said, "That sort of stuck in my craw, as to, why not do something about it?"

✷ ✷ ✷ ✷ ✷ ✷ ✷ ✷ ✷ ✷ ✷ ✷ ✷ ✷ ✷

Vivian Burey—known to her friends as Buster—was a seventeen-year-old freshman at the University of Pennsylvania when she saw Thurgood for the first time. He was a senior at Lincoln University, and both were attending a dinner party in Philadelphia. Buster noticed Thurgood, but "he was so busy arguing and debating with everyone at the table" that he didn't give her a second glance. Later, when they both attended an ice cream social near Buster's parents' church, Thurgood evidently did less arguing, because this time he noticed her—and he fell instantly in love.

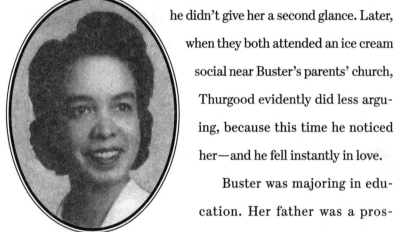

Vivian "Buster" Burey

Buster was majoring in education. Her father was a prosperous caterer for Philadelphia hotels. Like Thurgood, she had a heightened sense of the injustices perpetrated on African Americans. They began dating. They'd known each other for only a few months when they decided to get married. Norma tried to dissuade them. She thought they were too young and too poor.

"First we decided to get married five years after I graduated," Thurgood said, "then three, then one, and then we finally did it just before I started my last semester." Buster's sister had recently eloped, and Buster's parents were afraid she might do the same, so they consented to the marriage.

The wedding was held on September 4, 1929, at the Cherry Memorial Baptist Church in Philadelphia, followed by a reception at Buster's parents' home. The newlyweds moved into a small apartment not far from Lincoln. Buster worked as a secretary. Now that Thurgood was married, he settled down and gave up partying and gallivanting around. He didn't even rejoin the debate team. He studied harder than he'd ever studied before and raised his grade point average. He took so many classes that he was able to finish all of his coursework by the end of the semester, freeing up a semester before graduation to work and earn the money for law school tuition. During the semester he was free from classes, he and Buster lived with her parents in Philadelphia and he worked as a bellhop and a waiter.

In June of 1930, Thurgood was one of sixteen students to graduate from Lincoln with honors. He wanted to go to the University of Maryland School of Law. Tuition was low, and the school wasn't far from his parents' house, so he and Buster could live with them and he'd have an easy commute. But the University of Maryland didn't accept African American students.

There were a few high-quality northern universities that accepted African Americans, but they were too expensive. Thurgood called several lawyers in Baltimore to see if there was anything he could do to get into Maryland's law school. Each lawyer he spoke to gave him the same answer: There was nothing to be done. Enraged, Thurgood railed against the University of Maryland. He vowed that one day he'd get even.

His only option was Howard Law School for African Americans in Washington, D.C. "Howard Law was known as a 'dummy's retreat,'" he said later, "because the only people that went there were those who couldn't get in any other school."

The problem was that Thurgood didn't even have the money to cover Howard's tuition. His savings from working for a semester weren't enough. His mother had been paying his brother's way through medical school, and she had nothing left. Thurgood therefore planned to take off a year before law school so he could work to save his tuition money. Norma, though, said she couldn't bear to think of her college-educated son waiting tables, so she pawned her wedding and engagement rings to get the money for his first year's tuition. Thurgood didn't find out until years later how she had gotten the money.

3

Top Man in the Class

"I never worked hard until I got to the Howard Law School and met Charlie Houston . . . I saw this man's dedication, his vision, his willingness to sacrifice, and I told myself, 'You either shape up or ship out.' When you are being challenged by a great human being, you know that you can't ship out."

— Thurgood Marshall

n Thurgood's first day of classes at Howard Law School, he and thirty-five other men in his entering class walked up the stone steps of the law school's brownstone building. They filed into a large first-floor room and took their seats.

The new dean, Charles Hamilton Houston, stood at the front of the room, looking them over. Houston was a stern, dignified, imposing man with clipped short hair. He wore a formal woolen suit. He didn't offer a warm welcome. Instead he warned the entering class that he was making a few changes. He intended to transform Howard Law School into a serious, rigorous academic institution. The school would no longer put up with students who were not completely dedicated to their studies. He didn't care how well they had done in college; he would flunk them out if their work fell below his standards.

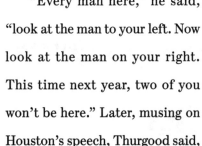

Charles Hamilton Houston, 1939

"Every man here," he said, "look at the man to your left. Now look at the man on your right. This time next year, two of you won't be here." Later, musing on Houston's speech, Thurgood said, "Well, you stopped to think, if he had said *one* of you, the odds wouldn't be so bad; but two out of three, that's murder!"

Houston went on to tell the first-year class, "I'll never be satisfied until I go to one of those dances up on the hill on the campus and see everybody having fun with all my law students sitting around the sides reading law books."

From that day forward, Thurgood applied himself 100 percent to his schoolwork. "I'd got the horsing around out of my system," he said, "and I'd heard law books were to dig in. So I dug, way deep."

He and Buster lived with his parents in Baltimore. Each morning he left the house by 5:00 a.m. to get to class on time. With his bag of books slung over his shoulder, he walked to the station and caught the early commuter train to Washington, D.C. From the station in Washington, he walked to his classes at 420 5th Street, in the northwest part of the city.

He was thrilled and inspired by the lectures, the law, the ideas, and the debates. "This was what I wanted to do for as long as I lived," he said. "I was at it twenty hours a day, seven days a week." Sometimes he slipped away from school to watch oral arguments in front of the Supreme Court. He felt particularly inspired watching John W. Davis, a Virginian, who frequently argued at the high court. Davis was a master in the courtroom. "Every time Davis argued," Thurgood said, "I'd ask myself, will I ever, ever . . . ?' and every time I had to answer, 'No, never.'"

Howard Law School's new dean, Charles Houston, was a legend in legal circles. Houston, the son of one of D.C.'s few prominent African American lawyers, had graduated high school at the age of fifteen. After a privileged upbringing, he attended

While a law student, Thurgood Marshall often listened to Supreme Court arguments. Pictured here is the interior of the Supreme Court.

the mostly white Amherst College. He responded to the racism of his classmates by being disciplined, hardworking, and aloof. He was a brilliant student and graduated from Amherst at the top of his class. He then joined the army and served in Europe in World War I. He had no legal training, but when he found that African Americans in the army were often convicted on flimsy charges without evidence, he figured out how to give them legal assistance. The experiences made him want to be a lawyer like his own father.

When the war ended in 1919, he enrolled in the Harvard Law School and faced the openly racist attitudes of many of his classmates. He excelled and became the first African American student to edit the *Harvard Law Review*, a top honor. He earned his law degree in 1922. Harvard offered him a scholarship to work toward a doctorate in law. He studied for a while in Spain. When he earned his doctorate, he was the best-educated African American lawyer in America.

Burning inside of Houston was pent-up rage at the injustices suffered by African Americans in America. A few African Americans succeeded: Poets Langston Hughes and Countee Cullen were widely read, and musicians Louis Armstrong, Duke Ellington, and Bill "Bojangles" Robinson achieved wide fame, but the statistics from a 1928 government report about life for most African Americans in America were grim. Whites lived an average of fourteen years longer than African Americans. There was one hospital bed available for an African American person for every 139 beds available to whites. Blacks were excluded from unions, and many white employers refused to hire them. In most places, schools for African Americans were so inferior to schools for whites that African Americans had little hope of lifting themselves from poverty. Houston understood that as a result of Jim Crow laws, racism was becoming institutionalized. The longer it went on and the deeper it sank into the American consciousness, the harder it would be to reverse.

Houston spent a year working at his father's law firm in Washington, D.C. Then, in 1933, the year Thurgood entered law school, Houston accepted the post of dean of Howard Law School. Houston was not only determined to improve Howard Law School, he was also "hell-bent on establishing a cadre of Negro lawyers dedicated to fighting for equal rights," Thurgood explained later. "This was done for a two-fold purpose. One was to do something for Negroes as such, and the other was to raise the image of the Negro lawyer. In those days, it wasn't high. There were no more than about ten prominent Negro lawyers in the late thirties, in the whole country."

Houston believed a lawyer was either a social engineer or a parasite. He told his students, "Men, you've got to be social engineers. We've got to turn this whole thing around. And the black man has got to do it; nobody's going to do it for you." Because everything a lawyer did was public, he demanded perfection. "The difference between law and other professions, like medicine," Houston said, "is the doctors bury their mistakes, but the lawyer's mistakes are made public. You've got to go out and compete with the other man, and you've got to be better than he is."

Later Marshall said that Houston insisted on such high standards that "He rightfully earned such beautiful phrases that we lovingly called him: Cement Drawers, Iron Pants, and a few other nice names." Under Houston's exacting standards, Thurgood's class shrank rapidly. Some found the work too demanding. Others were asked to leave because of low grades. During Thurgood's first year, the class went from thirty-five students to fewer than twenty.

Thurgood excelled in the first-year moot court competition. (Moot court is a mock courtroom where students practice trying cases. Often a sitting judge is invited to preside.) His legal research professor, William Hastie, said Thurgood was the most gifted first-year law student he ever taught. Thurgood finished his first year with the best grades in his class. "I came out top man," he said.

Thurgood spent the summer after his first year working as a waiter. His parents' house had become crowded by then. Aubrey had finished medical school, gotten married, and moved in with his wife, Sadie. He was working as a low-paid intern at Provident Hospital and hoped to be able to open a private medical practice. Sadie and Norma both worked as schoolteachers. Buster was a store clerk. Helen Prince, Sadie's mother, had also moved in with them. Within the year, Sadie had a baby named William Aubrey Jr. The house had a single bathroom. As was to be expected, there were squabbles. William was again out of a job, which increased the tension in the house. Thurgood avoided the family quarrels by leaving early each morning and returning late at night.

William Hastie, circa 1940

Thurgood in the law school library as a student librarian. Thurgood is behind the desk in the library talking to Oliver Hill, his closest friend in law school.

By the time Thurgood started his second year of law school, Charles Houston had achieved one of his goals for the school: He had lifted the academic standards high enough so that the school won its American Bar Association accreditation. He then lined up a roster of nationally known speakers.

Because Thurgood had finished his first year at the top of the class, he was rewarded with the single paid student position in the school: assistant, a job reserved for the highest-achieving student. The job paid half of his tuition. "In the library," he said, "as a student librarian, I didn't have anything to do but watch over the law books, so in my spare time, I read them. And that didn't hurt."

Thurgood's second-year grades, too, were stellar. By the time he began his third and final year of law school, the size of the class had shrunk to fewer than ten students. Only six would graduate. Houston treated the few remaining students "as if they were partners in an elite black law firm."

Supreme Court Justice Felix Frankfurter had been one of Houston's law school professors. When the NAACP wanted to devise a legal strategy for achieving civil rights for African Americans, they asked Justice Frankfurter to recommend someone who could help. Justice Frankfurter sent them to Charles Houston.

Houston called together his third-year students and put the problem to them. "We started sitting around with Charles Houston and William H. Hastie," Thurgood said, "and we began to work out this attack on the segregated school system. We talked about it. We did research on it. We studied it." They agreed that school segregation was the root of the problem for African Americans. If African Americans and whites attended the same schools, whites would be forced to interact with African Americans, and many of the racial stereotypes would disappear. If the two races attended school together, the smart African American children would be able to rise as high as the smart white children. Equality, they concluded, must begin in the schools.

They knew there was no way to persuade elected officials to get behind integration, particularly in the South. The reality was that elected officials answered to the voters, and the majority of voters were opposed to ending segregation. Part of the problem was that there were laws all over the South and elsewhere making it difficult for African Americans to vote. There were places where entire African American communities were prevented from voting. Thus, a cycle: Those who were oppressed could not vote against the laws, so it was hard for movements advocating reform of race-based laws to win a majority of voters.

Charles Houston believed that the place to attack segregation was in the courts, where federal judges were appointed for life and thus didn't answer to the voters. Moreover, judges— who were themselves lawyers—would be easier to persuade than politicians. The problem was the Supreme Court's decision in *Plessy v. Ferguson*, which stood like an impenetrable barrier.

In 1890, Louisiana passed a law making it illegal for any person with African heritage to ride in the same railroad cars as white people. Immediately after the law was passed, a group of concerned citizens, both African American and white, formed an organization dedicated to seeing the law repealed. Homer Plessy, a resident of New Orleans and an African American, became the group's most famous member.

On June 7, 1892, Plessy bought a train ticket and boarded the whites-only car. Railroad security had been alerted beforehand that Plessy would break the law. Plessy and the group wanted the arrest to be orderly. Shortly after the whistle blew and the train inched forward, conductor J. J. Dowling entered the car and asked Plessy if he was a colored man. His skin was so light it was difficult to tell. Plessy said he was. Dowling ordered him into the colored car. Plessy refused. A detective forcibly removed Plessy from the train and arrested him.

Plessy was found guilty and fined twenty-five dollars. He appealed his case to the United States Supreme Court, arguing that Louisiana's law violated the equal protection clause of the Fourteenth Amendment.

The pertinent portion of the Fourteenth Amendment states the following:

> *No state shall make or enforce any law which shall abridge the privileges or immunities of citizens of the United States; nor shall any state deprive any person of life, liberty, or property, without due process of law; nor deny to any person within its jurisdiction the equal protection of the laws.*

The Supreme Court—which consisted mostly of justices who approved of segregation and were sympathetic to the former Confederacy—ruled against Plessy, holding that segregation was permissible under the equal protection clause as long as the separate facilities were equal. "Laws permitting, and even requiring their separation . . . do not necessarily imply the inferiority of either race to the other," said the Supreme Court, thereby ushering in the Jim Crow era.

The difficulty facing Charles Houston and his students was that once the Supreme Court interprets the Constitution, there are only two ways to reverse the decision. The first is to amend the Constitution, a long and laborious process which requires two-thirds of the states to agree. Given how many states embraced the values of the former Confederacy, that was not realistic.

The second is to persuade the Supreme Court to overrule itself. Persuading the Court to overrule itself was also problematic, because some of the current justices approved of segregation, and because of the concept of legal precedent: When the Supreme Court makes a ruling, the case becomes *precedent* for future cases. This means that the case becomes like a rule that future courts must follow. A bedrock of the American legal system is stare decisis (pronounced *stairy de-sises*), which literally means "to stand by things decided." Once a court issues an important ruling, people and legislatures depend on the ruling. The ruling becomes part of the fabric of the society. If a court overrules itself too often, there can be no stability. The Supreme Court has said that stare decisis "promotes the even-handed, predicable, and consistent development of legal principles, fosters reliance on judicial decisions, and contributes to the . . . integrity of the judicial process." In fact, the Court has said it's more important for a rule of law to be settled than to be settled right.

After the Supreme Court's ruling in *Plessy v. Ferguson*, communities throughout the United States built entire social, legal, and educational systems based on the *Plessy* ruling that segregation was constitutional.

Thus—as Charles Houston understood—*Plessy* was precisely the kind of case the Supreme Court would be reluctant to overrule.

✳ ✳ ✳ ✳ ✳ ✳ ✳ ✳ ✳ ✳ ✳ ✳ ✳ ✳ ✳

As Thurgood was nearing the end of his third year, Harvard University offered him a scholarship to earn a doctorate in law. He turned it down. He was tired of being in school. "I couldn't wait to get out and practice," he said.

Thurgood was the only student in his law school class of six to graduate cum laude, with honors. He took the Maryland bar exam—the test that allowed a person to be licensed to practice law. The exam had a pass rate of 50 percent.

He was nervously waiting for his results when Houston invited him to take a trip into the Deep South to investigate conditions in the segregated schools. Houston saw the trip as a fact-finding mission. He hoped to collect enough documentation to help with a legal assault on segregation. Thurgood leaped at the chance. Both Thurgood and Houston had to listen to panicked family members warning them about how dangerous it was for two African American men with Yankee accents to travel through the South. Friends and family gave them phone numbers of friends and family members who would house them. African Americans were not allowed in hotels, so the only way to travel was to stay in private homes.

Thurgood and Houston packed a camera, a typewriter, notebooks, pens, and pencils. They wouldn't be allowed to eat in restaurants, so they carried bags of fruit and other food. They drove through Virginia and the Carolinas, Tennessee, and into Mississippi, where they saw cotton fields reaching to the horizon. During the long drives, Thurgood and Houston talked. By this time, they were on a first-name basis. They talked about the evils of segregation and how the courts might be used to achieve racial equality.

They stopped along the way to inspect schools and speak to African American educators and parents. What they found was appalling, grinding poverty. The worst of the schools for white children were better than the best of the schools for African Americans.

They saw that African American children in the Deep South were entirely cut off from white America. They couldn't even step into a public facility. In some places, it was simply impossible for African American children to attend school past third or fourth grade, because after that children were old enough to pick cotton in the fields. White employers and owners of the land often made sure that if every able-bodied person was not in the fields picking, the workers would not earn enough for food and would starve.

African American school, Mississippi, 1921

African American school, Virginia, 1937

Marshall was touched by how desperately parents hungered for education for their children.

In Mississippi, Thurgood and Houston were threatened by angry whites who didn't want two African American men coming around taking pictures of their schools. They were in so much danger in Mississippi that the local NAACP hired a funeral hearse with two riflemen to ride behind them for protection.

Soon after they returned to Baltimore, Thurgood learned that he had passed the bar exam. On October 11, 1933, he traveled to Annapolis to take his oath of office. He was now Mr. Marshall, attorney at law.

4

The Equalization Strategy

"In recognizing the humanity of our fellow human beings, we pay ourselves the highest tribute."
— Thurgood Marshall

hurgood Marshall had limited employment options. Wall Street law firms refused to hire African Americans. The most prestigious work available to new law school graduates, clerking for federal judges, was off limits. Government work, too, was closed to him. Marshall got the idea to ask Warner McGuinn, Baltimore's most successful African American lawyer, for a job. It didn't go well. "Young man," McGuinn said, cutting Marshall off before he could make his request, "you can save your time, and you can save my ears. Forget it. I've known you since you were born, and I have carefully watched your progress in law school. It was unbelievably good. You're going to practice by yourself and get your brains kicked out, and then come back to me and we'll talk."

Marshall walked away angry. He figured he'd have to open his own law office. He wanted to be in the heart of Baltimore's business district, but he couldn't find someone willing to rent office space to him. All the African American lawyers in Baltimore rented office space at least four blocks north of the central business district. At last he met Adolph Ginsberg, a white commercial landlord willing to rent him office space in the Phoenix Building, a building with a prime business location.

Marshall joined several other African American lawyers and rented four rooms in the Phoenix Building. One of them was another new lawyer, William Alfred Carroll Hughes Jr. Another was Warner McGuinn. Thurgood got over his anger at being rebuffed for a job when McGuinn went out of his way to help Marshall get started. McGuinn even sent Marshall a few clients.

The lawyers pooled their money to hire a secretary. Later they were able to hire a second one. Marshall's office consisted of a desk that McGuinn lent him, a phone, and a rug his parents gave him from their living room. Mostly he had nothing to do.

The Equalization Strategy

The problem was that the year was 1933, it was the height of the Great Depression, and there wasn't much work for anyone.

The Great Depression, which started in 1929 and lasted until about 1939, was a time of widespread poverty and unemployment. Twenty percent of the entire workforce in Baltimore was unemployed. The rate was higher among African Americans. Many families were unable to afford basics like food and housing. Charities set up soup kitchens and breadlines to give free food to the hungry.

✴ ✴ ✴ ✴ ✴ ✴ ✴ ✴ ✴ ✴ ✴ ✴ ✴ ✴ ✴

From Thurgood's office window, he could see the breadlines. During his first year in practice, he didn't earn enough to cover his office expenses. He wondered if he'd made a mistake in turning down Harvard's scholarship for a doctorate in law.

He often worked for free when his clients couldn't pay. One day an African American woman came to see him. She had a

country accent and wore a tattered red skirt. She told Marshall she had legal troubles, but "I don't have a nickel." Marshall asked how she happened to pick him. She said, "Well, down in North Carolina in my little town, when we have a legal problem, we go to the judge, and he helps us out." When she came to Baltimore and needed legal help, she went to see a judge, who sent her to Marshall, saying, "He's a freebie lawyer, he'll do it for you for nothing." Marshall handled her case. Later he laughed when he told the story and said, "I've got to stop that crap right now." But he didn't. He joked about how working without pay "wasn't a good way to make a living," but when clients had no money, he did the work for free.

He took anything that came his way. He handled divorces and personal injury cases. He represented small businesses in routine matters. He defended African Americans accused of crimes. He landed his biggest client—John Murphy, treasurer of the *Afro-American*, the nation's largest African American newspaper chain—when Murphy had a spat with his longtime lawyer, Warner McGuinn. McGuinn referred Murphy to Marshall. He told Marshall, "Go ahead. You'll [mess] it up, and it'll come back to me anyhow." Marshall did not mess it up, and he gained an important client.

Depression-era breadlines

Buster took a job at a catalog company. She worked for two weeks, and then her employer refused to pay her. She wanted Thurgood to sue her employer for the money he owed her, but he refused, explaining that it would be a waste of time because the guy probably didn't have any money. So Buster went to the courthouse and filled out the paperwork herself. She not only asked for the money her employer owed her, she also itemized what he owed other people and sued for them to get their money, too. The judge asked her why her husband wasn't handling the matter for her. She said he was too busy trying to find paying clients. The judge laughed. She won her case and collected her money. So did the others.

★ ★ ★ ★ ★ ★ ★ ★ ★ ★ ★ ★ ★ ★ ★

Buster and Marshall had no children. Several times Buster became pregnant, but each time she miscarried the child, leaving both her and Marshall devastated. Buster spent her spare time after work as a social and political activist. She joined picket lines when African American workers demanded their rights—a dangerous thing to do in the mid-1930s.

Marshall did his part for social causes by giving free legal advice to the local chapter of the NAACP and other activist groups. One group wanted to boycott stores that catered to

African Americans but refused to hire African American clerks. When they came to Marshall for advice, he visited the police commissioner and explained exactly what the protesters planned to do. After the police approved of the plan, he told the protesters they could go ahead. Marshall wasn't taking any chances.

Marshall and Houston stayed in close touch and continued discussing the best way to attack racial segregation. One of Houston's friends and colleagues, the Harvard-educated Nathan Margold, suggested that they shouldn't attack segregation itself. The plan could backfire on them by prompting the Supreme Court to reaffirm its ruling in *Plessy v. Ferguson*, thus making it even harder to overturn.

Margold thought they should insist that states live up to the requirement in *Plessy v. Ferguson* and provide truly equal schools. His idea was that if states and local communities were forced to provide schools for African Americans that were as good as the school for whites, they would understand that the duplication in costs—separate buildings, separate labs, separate gyms, etc.— would not be worth it. Marshall thought the idea was a good one. "The South would go broke paying for truly equal dual systems," he said. Southern officials would have to choose between going broke or letting African Americans into schools for whites.

Houston and Marshall refined Margold's ideas into what they called their "equalization strategy." They would file lawsuits demanding that communities either provide equal facilities for African Americans or admit them to white institutions. They would start with public schools, because the Fourteenth Amendment specifically applied to states, and public schools were run by local governments. At the same time, they would lay the groundwork for the next step—an actual challenge to *Plessy v. Ferguson.*

Marshall thought it was best to begin with the professional schools. Providing separate but equal elementary school classrooms was much easier than providing separate but equal medical schools or law schools. A state couldn't possibly duplicate the facilities, libraries, laboratories, and faculty of a medical or law school. If only one African American applied, it would be absurd to build a separate but equal school, so the single African American student would have to be admitted to the all-white school. This would break the barrier in a way least alarming to the white population. Whites were more likely to respond with fury to mixing younger children. Moreover, law schools and professional schools at the time were almost entirely male. Demanding that a fully qualified African American male student be admitted to an all-male law school or medical school was less likely to create an uproar.

The Equalization Strategy

Their plan was to be careful not to push for too much too soon. They didn't want to ignite a backlash. Instead, they would chip away at the edges of segregation. Their goal was to educate judges about the evils of segregation and persuade them that separate but equal was not a workable doctrine. They wanted to get the public accustomed to the idea of integration and raise awareness that segregation was based on hatred and racism.

In 1933, several African American men applied to the University of Maryland law school and were turned down. There was talk among Washington, D.C., lawyers about suing the University of Maryland to force the university to admit them. Marshall was itching to sue the University of Maryland, but he needed resources, which he didn't have. He was also concerned that someone would sue the university but not do it well and make it harder for others later. He thought he and Houston should be the ones to handle it.

"Dear Charlie," he wrote in January 1934. "Trust you had a good Christmas, etc. I hate to worry you so much about this University of Maryland case. When are we to get together on it? Things are very slow right now, and I would like very much to get started as soon as possible." Houston responded that he, too, was eager to get started. The first thing they needed was a good plaintiff.

There are two parties to a lawsuit: the plaintiff and the defendant. The plaintiff brings the lawsuit against the defendant. The standing requirement and the case and controversy clause of the United States Constitution limit who can be a plaintiff and bring a lawsuit.

Article III sets forth the scope and limits of the judicial branch. (The Constitution has three articles: Article I describes the legislative branch, Article II the executive branch, and Article III the judicial branch.)

One important function of the Constitution is to limit the power of each branch. To limit the power of judges, Article III, Section 2 forbids courts from giving advice. Judges cannot say in advance how a law can or should be interpreted. They cannot issue rulings without an actual case and controversy, and they must rule only on the particular facts before them.

From these concepts, the Supreme Court has held that only a plaintiff with standing can bring a case, meaning that the plaintiff must have been injured or have a personal stake in the outcome.

The Equalization Strategy

Marshall and Houston needed a plaintiff who was qualified for admission and who was willing to apply, get rejected, and then sue the university.

The perfect plaintiff, Donald Gaines Murray, approached one of Marshall's colleagues, William Gosnell, looking for help. Murray was a twenty-two-year-old recent graduate from Amherst College. Amherst was a top-notch college, and Murray had stellar grades. Murray was intelligent, well spoken, and personable. He wanted to study law. In particular, he wanted to go to the University of Maryland.

Murray—with Marshall's guidance—wrote a letter to the law school asking for an application. Murray received a chilly response from Raymond Pearson, the president of the university. First Pearson suggested that Murray apply to the Princess Anne Academy, which Pearson called "a separate institution of higher learning for the education of Negroes." The problem with this option was that the Princess Anne Academy was, at best, equivalent to the first two years of a regular college.

The second option Pearson offered Murray was to apply for an out-of-state tuition grant. "In order to insure equality of opportunity for all citizens of this state," Pearson wrote, the state had made available partial scholarships for students who wished to take professional courses not offered by the Princess Anne Academy. The scholarship fund was to allow the students to take the courses in an out-of-state university that admitted African Americans. The first problem was that there was no guarantee the student could find an out-of-state university willing to take them. The second problem was that the scholarship fund, which had been hurriedly set up, was inadequate to cover out-of-state expenses. As a third option, Pearson suggested that Murray apply to Howard University.

Marshall helped Murray draft a letter back to Pearson, stressing that Murray was qualified for admission to the University of Maryland. Naturally, this letter was ignored. Murray obtained an application, which he filled out and submitted to the law school. Within a few weeks, the university registrar returned his application with a note informing him that the university did not accept African American students except to the Princess Anne Academy.

Marshall, Gosnell, and Houston were ready to file Murray's lawsuit. The basis of their lawsuit was that the University of Maryland violated the equal protection clause of the Fourteenth Amendment by failing to provide a state law school for African Americans equivalent to the school for whites.

1935: Marshall with Donald Gaines Murray and Charles Houston at a table preparing for the trial

They filed the paperwork on April 20, 1935. They expected to lose their trial and take their case to a higher court on appeal.

The trial began on June 18. Houston was the lead lawyer. Houston, Marshall, and Murray sat at the plaintiff's table. All three wore double-breasted wool suits with their handkerchiefs folded neatly in their breast pockets and their white shirts starched and ironed. Marshall's parents were in the courtroom to watch.

Raymond Pearson, president of the university, took the

stand. He tried to argue that the Princess Anne Academy offered substantially the same education as the law school. Houston easily made mincemeat of his arguments, presenting evidence about the caliber of the faculty and course offerings. The plaintiff's third witness was Roger Howell, dean of the University of Maryland law school, who confirmed that a large part of the law school's curriculum focused on Maryland law.

When it was Thurgood Marshall's turn to take over, he made the constitutional arguments, assuring the court that in not providing a separate but equal education for African American law students, the state was in violation of the Constitution as interpreted by the Supreme Court in *Plessy v. Ferguson.* Marshall— the champion debater and good talker—performed brilliantly,

The Tenth Amendment states simply that, "The powers not delegated to the United States by the Constitution, nor prohibited by it to the States, are reserved to the States respectively, or to the people."

The states' rights argument goes like this: There is nothing in the Constitution giving the federal government particularly compared to the defense lawyer, state attorney Charles LeViness, who, when his turn came to speak, bungled his way through the case law. LeViness, however, was confident that he'd prevail. In his mind, the idea that a judge could tell a local government how to run its schools was absurd and unconstitutional under the Tenth Amendment.

* * * * * * * * * * * * * * *

On June 25, the court was ready with an announcement. The judge told a stunned audience that he was issuing a writ of mandamus—an order from a court to a government official ordering the official to properly fulfill his or her duties. The writ ordered the University of Maryland School of Law to admit Donald Murray.

power over local schools. Therefore, local communities should be able to manage their schools any way they choose. The problem with relying on the Tenth Amendment to justify segregation is that the Fourteenth Amendment requires that states provide all persons with "equal protection of the laws."

After the court announced its decision, Charles LeViness, state attorney, asked to speak. He said, "I wish to be quoted as saying that I hope that Mr. Murray leads the class in the law school."

★ ★ ★ ★ ★ ★ ★ ★ ★ ★ ★ ★ ★ ★

Word of the victory spread quickly. Marshall and Houston were instant heroes in Baltimore's African American and liberal communities. Walter White, executive secretary of the NAACP, called the victory "epoch making." Houston warned that the road ahead was a difficult one. He wrote an article entitled "Don't Shout Too Soon," in which he warned that the victory in the University of Maryland test case did not mean the battle for education equality for African Americans was over. In fact, it was just getting started.

The strategy to start with law schools and professional schools—and a client like Donald Murray—was proven wise when the influential columnist for the *Baltimore Evening Sun*, H. L. Mencken, wrote his commentary on the case. Mencken said that while he was opposed to mixing races in schools, there was no reason for those at the law school at the University of Maryland to object "to the presence among them of a self-respecting and ambitious young Afro-American, well prepared for his studies by four years of hard work in a class A college." Moreover, he noted that law students were not children or "adolescents going through the ordinary college mill and eager only to dance and [kiss]."

The state of Maryland said it would appeal.

Appeals take time. The lawyers must file paperwork with the court of appeals (appellate court), and write lengthy briefs presenting their facts and arguments. Then the court schedules oral arguments, which consist of a lawyer representing each side standing at podiums before a panel of appellate judges, called justices, and presenting their cases and answering questions. The appellate court in Maryland would not be able to hear arguments in Donald Murray's case until October, after the start of the school term. There was, therefore, nothing to stop Murray from becoming the first African American student to enroll in the University of Maryland School of Law.

Marshall and Houston both received threatening letters from the Ku Klux Klan, which they ignored. Marshall accompanied Murray to the school in September for the start of classes. The dean suggested that Murray sit apart from the white students. Marshall and Murray walked around campus until they found two white students willing to tell the dean they didn't mind

Thurgood Marshall
as a young lawyer, 1935

sitting next to Murray. Throughout his first day, Murray's new classmates shook his hand, wished him well, and offered him help or support should he need it. The *Afro-American* reported that Murray's classmates were "exceedingly cordial and so were professors."

✴ ✴ ✴ ✴ ✴ ✴ ✴ ✴ ✴ ✴ ✴ ✴ ✴ ✴ ✴

Murray won his appeal, so he was able to remain in the law school. After earning his degree and passing the bar exam, Donald Murray practiced law in Baltimore and eventually became a partner in the firm of Douglass, Perkins and Murray. He worked with the NAACP on several cases attacking racial segregation in schools.

5

A Social Engineer

*"A child born to a black mother in a state like Mississippi . . .
has exactly the same rights as a white baby born to the wealthiest
person in the United States. It's not true, but I challenge
anyone to say it is not a goal worth fighting for."*
— *Thurgood Marshall*

The ruling in *Murray v. Pearson* sent panic waves through segregationists in Maryland and elsewhere. Other communities, afraid of being hit with similar lawsuits, raised their budgets for educational facilities for African American schools. The state of Maryland gave the state teachers' college for African American students at Bowie money for a new building. The state also gave a private school for African Americans in Baltimore a grant to build a new gymnasium. The Richmond *Times-Dispatch* urged Virginia to take similar steps. The

Times-Dispatch also warned that the moment an African American student entered the University of Virginia, the door would be opened to miscegenation (mixing of the races through marriage).

Houston left his position as dean of Howard Law School and became full-time special counsel to the NAACP. He and Marshall selected their next target: the Baltimore high schools. In Baltimore County—the area that formed an arc around the city of Baltimore to the east, north, and west—there were ten high schools for whites and none for African Americans, even though African Americans made up 10 percent of the population. African American students who wanted to continue their education were given a written test to see if they qualified. If they passed, they were admitted to the colored high school in Baltimore, but they were not offered public transportation, which often made it impossible for rural children to attend. White students didn't have to take a test. They were automatically admitted to high school.

The parents of a seventh-grade girl, Margaret Williams, approached the NAACP for help. Margaret hadn't passed the test, but her family was determined to see her get a high school education. Marshall and Houston sued the school district demanding that Margaret Williams be admitted to the high school for whites in her neighborhood.

Marshall with possible plaintiffs. Margaret Williams, who became a plaintiff, is on the right.

Marshall was the lead attorney at the trial. He had three lawyers as his support: one of his former law professors, Leon Andrew Ransom; Oliver Hill, who had been his closest friend in law school; and Edward Lovett, a Washington, D.C., lawyer in private practice.

The school board argued that admitting an African American

girl to a white high school would "break down the traits of the state of Maryland." Marshall and his team argued that refusing to admit her to the white high school violated her rights under the Fourteenth Amendment.

The court ruled against Margaret Williams, holding that it was up to the county board of education to determine the requirements for students attending their schools. Marshall appealed. The appellate court also ruled against her on the grounds that they had requested the wrong remedy: They should have demanded that the county pay for the plaintiff to attend the colored high school in Baltimore without the requirement of passing an exam.

Marshall and Houston understood they had reached for too much too fast. The loss was a painful disappointment. The NAACP, though, was pleased with Marshall's work. Walter White, the NAACP's executive secretary, began using Marshall as the organization's point man in Washington.

* * * * * * * * * * * * * * *

Houston went to Missouri, where a man named Lloyd Gaines had asked the NAACP for help. Gaines was twenty-five years old, a resident of St. Louis, Missouri, and he

Lloyd Gaines, circa 1930

wanted to go to law school. He had graduated from Lincoln University, Missouri's state college for African Americans.

In 1935, Gaines applied to the University of Missouri School of Law, located in Columbia, Missouri, but the university refused to consider his application because he was African American. The university told him that he could apply to Lincoln and pursue a legal education there—though there was nothing like a law school at Lincoln—or he could apply to an out-of-state law school and the state of Missouri would cover his tuition.

Houston and the local NAACP lawyers in Missouri worked up the case following the precedent Marshall and Houston had established in Murray's Maryland case. They filed their claim in the Boone County Courthouse, asking for a writ of mandamus to the registrar of the University of Missouri ordering the law school to admit Gaines. Houston went to Missouri to serve as the trial lawyer.

Houston hoped for a sizable African American audience to

show support for the lawsuit, but there were almost no African Americans in the courtroom. Two African Americans had recently been lynched nearby in Columbia, Missouri, so other people were too frightened to attend. The courtroom was filled with whites, though, many of them local farmers wearing overalls. The courtroom and facilities were not segregated. Houston said that during recess, some farmers "looked a little strange at us drinking out of the same fountain and using the same lavatories, but they did not say anything."

Houston sensed the outcome from the atmosphere in the courthouse. The whites in Boone County did not want an African American man in the state's law school. "It is beyond expectation that the court will decide in our favor," Houston wrote to the office, "so we had just as well get ready for the appeal."

✴ ✴ ✴ ✴ ✴ ✴ ✴ ✴ ✴ ✴ ✴ ✴ ✴ ✴ ✴

There was simply too much legal work for one person at the NAACP, so Charles Houston proposed adding another full-time lawyer. Walter White approved the plan. Houston immediately wrote to Marshall, "I don't know of anybody I would rather have in the office than you or anybody who can do a better job of research and preparation of cases."

Marshall said that when he received the letter, "I whooped and hollered so loud that Buster ran in to see if I was dying." Marshall was eager to be a full-time social engineer and tired of trying to scratch out a living in a private office. The job required relocating to New York. He wrote to White that "I will be indebted to you and Charlie for a long time to come for many reasons, one of which is that I have an opportunity now to do what I have always dreamed of doing."

★ ★ ★ ★ ★ ★ ★ ★ ★ ★ ★ ★ ★ ★

About this time, Aubrey was stricken by illness. At night, Marshall heard his brother coughing and hacking. Aubrey's body began to deteriorate. Shortly after Marshall accepted his new job, Aubrey was diagnosed with tuberculosis. The diagnosis crushed Aubrey and sent the family reeling in shock. The disease was often deadly and highly contagious. Aubrey was forced to close his medical practice, which threw the family into financial crisis. Aubrey's marriage was already shaky because of all the family quarrels. Sadie moved out and took their children to keep them from becoming infected.

The best hospitals for treating tuberculosis admitted only white people. Norma planned to care for Aubrey herself, even though William was only working intermittently, which meant that the family depended on her paycheck.

Marshall hesitated to move away from Baltimore to take a new job at such a time, but Norma insisted. The last thing she wanted was for one of her sons to pass up an employment opportunity. So, in Marshall's words, he and Buster "gathered up our rags and moved to New York." Initially they lived with Thurgood's aunt and uncle, Medi and Boots. Soon they were able to afford their own home, "a little apartment near the Polo Grounds," as Marshall later described it.

The NAACP headquarters were located at 69 Fifth Avenue. There was a flagpole holder outside one of their windows. Any time an African American person was lynched, the following day a flag announced to the city that A MAN WAS LYNCHED YESTERDAY. During the early- and mid-1930s, there were about ten lynchings per year, mostly in the Deep South. The killers were never brought to justice.

Marshall and Houston shared a small office. Marshall, who remained in awe of his former law school dean, felt flattered to be working by his side. Marshall worked as hard as he had in law school. Working so closely together highlighted the differences in their personalities. Houston was quiet, dignified, and formal.

Marshall was rambunctious, loud-voiced, and always ready to tell a joke. Marshall disliked formalities. By the end of the day, his shirt was usually untucked and his tie loosened. He exchanged stories with the secretaries and janitors. "Everyone loved Thurgood," said one NAACP official. "Where Houston was aloof, Marshall had the common touch. He had great energy and warmth."

Marshall spent much of his time traveling, gathering evidence, and meeting with potential plaintiffs. On one trip to North Carolina, he wrote, "School situation is terrible. Principal of elementary school is gardener and janitor for the county superintendent of schools and is a typical Uncle Tom." (*Uncle Tom* is a derisive term for African Americans who don't stand up for themselves but go along with whatever authority figures—white people—want.)

Marshall and Houston decided to attack the inequality in pay between white and African American teachers. Tackling pay rates for teachers was easier than attacking other manifestations of racism because teachers' pay was set by school boards and documented in writing. Finding plaintiffs, though, was not easy. Entire families often lived on a teacher's paycheck, and teachers were afraid they'd be fired in retaliation if they sued the school board.

Marshall drove around Maryland in his old Ford, talking to teachers and members of school boards. Eventually he found willing plaintiffs. He fought the battle for equal pay one county at a time, first suing the school board, then appealing when he lost.

By then Marshall had developed into a brilliant litigator with an exquisite sense of timing. From his days as a debater, he knew how to make a point through understatement. During one trial, a superintendent defended the pay inequity on the grounds that "his poorest white teacher was better than the best colored teacher." Marshall, astounded, allowed a beat of time pass. He then responded with a question: Why did African American teachers and not white teachers have to scrub the classroom floors? The superintendent said it was because scrubbing floors "had always been African Americans' work." Marshall didn't respond. Instead, he calmly took his seat, letting the outrageous remark hang unanswered, thereby highlighting the stark racism. The silence in the courtroom at that moment was electrifying. The strategy worked. The judge ruled for the African American teachers.

Eventually the governor and the Maryland legislature passed a law setting a single pay scale for African American and white teachers. Marshall suspected he had won simply because it was less expensive for Maryland to change the law than to keep fighting him in court.

★　★　★　★　★　★　★　★　★　★　★　★　★　★　★

One day Marshall was in his office going through stacks of newspapers when he happened upon a sensational story about an African American college president in Dallas, Texas. George F. Porter, who was fifty-five years old, had been called for jury duty three times. The first two times he presented himself at the Dallas courthouse, he was sent home because he was African American.

When Porter received his third summons, he entered the courtroom and insisted that he be put on a jury. One potential juror, enraged by his request, threatened to beat him up. A second grabbed him by the collar and dragged him through the halls of the courthouse. Porter was struggling to keep his balance when his attacker pushed him out the door and down the courthouse steps. He was scratched and bruised, but able to stand up. He walked back up the stairs and into the courtroom. The judge told him it was too late. The jury had already been empaneled.

Marshall thought it was just the kind of story that that would bring national attention to the "monstrous reality of second-class treatment given to black Americans even in a court of law." Houston agreed. So Marshall made plans to head down to Texas to see if he could get Porter placed on a jury.

When the Dallas chief of police learned that Marshall was coming to Dallas to investigate local jury practices, he called his top officers and told them that an African American lawyer was coming from New York to stir up trouble. He told the officers not to lay a hand on Thurgood Marshall because he planned to "personally take him out and kick the sh— out of him."

Marshall received a warning that the Dallas chief of police planned to shoot him on the spot. "I sort of considered the idea of having a bad cold or something and not going down there," Marshall said. He'd heard that the governor of Texas, James Allred, was a fair and decent man. So Marshall called Allred and explained the situation. "I give you my word," Allred said. "If you come down here, you will not be injured."

So Marshall went. Allred assigned a Texas ranger to protect Marshall. The ranger kept referring to Marshall as "boy," but Marshall soon learned that he was the "right man for the job." When the chief of police caught up with Marshall and shouted, "I've got you now!" Marshall was terrified. The ranger, though, calmly pulled his gun and pointed it at the chief of police. "Fella," he said, "just stay right where you are." The police chief didn't move. The ranger kept his gun pointed at the police chief as he and Marshall got into their car and drove away.

Marshall's visit resulted in nationwide publicity, which in turn put enormous pressure on the Dallas courthouse. The result was that within a few weeks of Marshall's arrival, an African American man, W. L. Dickson, was empaneled on a jury. Governor Allred assigned a ranger to protect Dickson.

★   ★   ★   ★   ★   ★   ★   ★   ★   ★   ★   ★   ★   ★

A ripple of excitement shot through the offices of the NAACP when the United States Supreme Court agreed to hear Lloyd Gaines's appeal from the Missouri ruling preventing him from enrolling in the University of Missouri School of Law. Unlike most other courts, the United States Supreme Court chooses which cases it will hear, and it has time to hear only a small fraction of the cases submitted for review. The Court tends to choose only cases of national importance. This would be the first time the United States Supreme Court would hear a racial segregation case since *Plessy v. Ferguson.*

Charles Houston argued the case in the Supreme Court.

A Social Engineer

He was careful not to attack or challenge segregation itself. His argument was simply that under the Court's ruling in *Plessy v. Ferguson*, Lloyd Gaines was entitled to a legal education equal to that offered to white residents of Missouri. If Missouri did not want to admit Gaines to the University of Missouri School of Law, the state of Missouri would simply have to build a law school for African Americans that offered the same quality of education. Attending school out-of-state was not good enough, because it wasn't equal: The University of Missouri focused on Missouri law, and Gaines intended to practice in St. Louis.

The Supreme Court issued its decision one month later. Chief Justice Hughes read the decision from the bench. Gaines won. The Supreme Court justices ruled 6–3 that Missouri either had to build a law school for African Americans equal in all respects to the law school for whites, or it had to admit Gaines to the University of Missouri School of Law.

It was a stunning victory. The win made it clear that equality was not satisfied by scholarships to study out of state. As Marshall later phrased it, "A state could not export its Fourteenth Amendment responsibilities." It was also clear to Marshall that this ruling—handed down from the United States Supreme

Court—would also apply to high schools and elementary schools. Moreover, there was no reason the ruling should be limited to schools. What about parks, and libraries, and public lavatories? Wouldn't any public place closed to African Americans fall under the same rule? The possibilities were enough to make a civil rights lawyer positively giddy.

6

Speaking Out

*"Where you see wrong or inequality or injustice,
speak out, because this is your country. This is your democracy—
make it—protect it—pass it on. You are ready. Go to it."*
—Thurgood Marshall

harles Houston announced that he was resigning his position as special counsel for the NAACP. He offered various reasons. One was that he'd experienced intermittent health issues since his service in the army, when he'd had a bout of tuberculosis. Another was overwork: He was on the verge of an exhaustion breakdown. He also found that conforming to an organization didn't suit him. He preferred to offer advice to NAACP lawyers from outside. "I am much more of an outside man than an inside man," he said. He intended to return to private practice.

Thurgood Marshall was promoted to lead special counsel of the NAACP. The first thing Marshall did was write a charter for what he called the Legal Defense Fund. Its mission was to "render legal aid gratuitously to such Negroes as may appear to be worthy." He helped raise money for his fund by giving talks.

Marshall cultivated a network of lawyers spread across the nation who were willing to take on cases to help African Americans in trouble. Creating such a network wasn't easy. There was a severe shortage of well-trained African American lawyers. Throughout much of the South, taking on civil rights cases was considered an act of defiance and was likely to result in being forced out of the practice of law or even run out of town. Simply joining the NAACP was dangerous and often seen as an act of defiance. Many local NAACP branches, therefore, operated in secrecy.

Marshall kept up his pressure on school systems, encouraging local NAACP branch offices to sue school districts to force them to provide equal facilities for African American students. While desegregation was the long-term goal, he took all kinds of cases. He sued southern sheriffs who arbitrarily and unfairly arrested African Americans. He demanded equal pay for African American teachers in Little Rock, Arkansas. He defended the voting rights of African Americans in South Carolina and Texas. He represented African American workers who were forced to work all day on Election Day without time to go to the polls, making it impossible for them to vote.

As he traveled, he was meticulous about obeying all local ordinances. He sat in the colored sections of buses and trains. He did as he was told by whites—except in the courtroom, where he boldly asserted the rights of all persons under the Constitution. He regularly received death threats. Someone asked him once if he was worried about being murdered by an angry mob. "If it happens," he said, "it happens."

He had one particularly memorable encounter in Mississippi. "I was out there on the train platform trying to look small," he said, "when this cold-eyed man with a gun on his hip came up. 'N—,' he said, 'I thought you outta know the sun ain't nevah set on a live N— in this town.'"

Marshall set aside his father's long-ago advice to settle the matter right then and there. Instead, "I wrapped up my constitutional rights in cellophane, tucked them in my hip pocket—and caught the next train."

★　★　★　★　★　★　★　★　★　★　★　★　★　★　★

By the late 1930s, America was coming out of the Great Depression. Credit for lifting the nation from the Depression was largely given to Democratic President Franklin D. Roosevelt's New Deal, a series of laws that gave the federal government power to intervene and make life better for people at the bottom of the economic hierarchy. The New Deal gave the nation a minimum wage, the forty-hour workweek, Social Security, the right to safety in the workplace, and one of the most far-reaching pieces of legislation, the G.I. Bill, which allowed returning soldiers the right to a government-paid college education. In the 1920s, only about 5 percent of American families could afford college for their children. The G.I. Bill allowed thousands of Americans to break the poverty cycle and enter the middle class.

African Americans benefited from these new programs, but as second-class citizens.

President Roosevelt viewed the dilemma of African Americans with compassion, but he was unwilling to abandon his alliance with white southern Democrats, who—since the time of the Civil War—had made up a majority of the Democratic Party. He did, however, take steps forward. His attorney general, Frank Murphy, set up the first Civil Rights government office. The War Department opened its ranks to African Americans, and William Hastie, Marshall's former professor at Howard Law School, was named as advisor. Later, Roosevelt would appoint Hastie as a federal judge in the Virgin Islands, making him the first African American federal judge.

Even more significant were changes happening on the Supreme Court. When Roosevelt took office in 1933, the Supreme Court was staunchly conservative. During Roosevelt's time in office, the Court—largely because of the justices Roosevelt appointed—was becoming more liberal and thus slightly more inclined to rule on behalf of African Americans seeking equal rights.

✷ ✷ ✷ ✷ ✷ ✷ ✷ ✷ ✷ ✷ ✷ ✷ ✷ ✷ ✷

One day in December 1939, a grisly murder rocked the small farming village of Fort Towson, Oklahoma. A killer broke into the home of a farmer and brutally murdered the man, his wife, and their four-year-old son. Miraculously, the nine-year-old

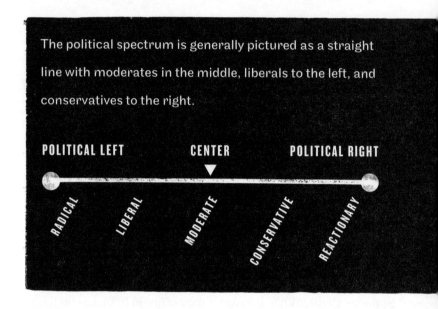

The political spectrum is generally pictured as a straight line with moderates in the middle, liberals to the left, and conservatives to the right.

POLITICAL LEFT   CENTER   POLITICAL RIGHT

RADICAL   LIBERAL   MODERATE   CONSERVATIVE   REACTIONARY

and his infant brother escaped by hiding in a closet. The family was white.

The perpetrators were soon caught: two white prisoners from a local prison farm. The killers confessed. The evidence of their guilt was overwhelming. This, however, did not calm the people of Oklahoma, who demanded to know why government officials had allowed such brutal killers to escape from prison, thus allowing them to kill again. The people blamed the government officials for the murders.

Governor Leon Phillips wanted to end the negative publicity as soon as possible, so he enlisted the help of a special

On the left side of the political spectrum, liberals are comfortable with change, and look for changes that they believe will improve society. Radicals want to bring about swift changes, looking eagerly ahead to what they believe will be a better world. On the political right, conservatives are less comfortable with change. They prefer stability and the status quo. Reactionaries feel something has been lost. They long for the past—a time, they believe, when the nation was great. Those in the middle, moderates, avoid both extremes.

investigator, Vernon Cheatwood, to come up with a solution. A big and brutal man, Mr. Cheatwood was known for his ability to extract confessions from any suspect. Cheatwood did some investigating and ordered the police to arrest W. D. Lyons, an African American man who had been hunting rabbits in the vicinity of the farmhouse the night of the murder.

Lyons denied having anything to do with the murder. Cheatwood and his officers held Lyons for forty-eight hours, beating him and depriving him of food and sleep. Lyons refused to confess. Then Cheatwood threw the bones of a dead baby into his lap and said with a growl, "There's the bones of the baby you burned up." Presumably the bones were either not those of a real baby, or they were those of a different baby. Lyons, described as superstitious, would have been deeply rattled to think bones were being thrown at him. He broke down completely. He tried to crawl away from the bones, but Cheatwood pushed them into his face. Lyons then confessed to the murder. "I was forced to," he said later. "I was beat with a blackjack, tortured all night

W. D. Lyons, arrested and handcuffed. Vernon Cheatwood is farthest to the right.

long—because I feared I would get some more torture." After he signed a confession, he was taken to the penitentiary.

When the torture ceased, he again denied having committed the murder, so he was taken to the basement and shown the electric chair where prisoners were executed. Guards bragged about how many African American men they had executed with it. Lyons overheard officers telling each other that they should hang and bury him right there. Shortly afterward, the officers got Lyons to sign a second confession.

A lawyer, a white man named Stanley Belden, was appointed to represent him. Beldon quickly concluded that Lyons was innocent. He asked Marshall to help. Marshall traveled by train to Oklahoma to conduct the trial. Angry whites were enraged by the idea of an "uppity New York Negro" lawyer coming to Oklahoma to "make trouble." Marshall received death threats. He spent each night of the trial in a different place. "I didn't want anyone, I mean anybody, to know that during that first night in Hugo I lay in bed sweating in fear. I think I remembered every lynching story that I had read about after World War One. I could see my body lying in some place where they let white kids out of Sunday School to come and look at me and rejoice."

The courtroom was filled with spectators, African American

and white, to watch an African American defense attorney face off against a white prosecutor. Lyons took the witness stand. He testified that an officer named Horton saw the police beating him. When Horton took the stand, he denied having seen any brutal whippings. Lyons looked him in the eye and said, "Oh, yes, you were there." Horton's face went white, and he shouted, "I stopped them from whipping you!" At that, the courtroom erupted.

Marshall took advantage of the moment to get Horton to concede that Lyons had been beaten by the police. When Cheatwood took the stand, Marshall got him to admit that he'd thrown the bones at Lyons. "I thought it would refresh his mind," Cheatwood said. A witness confirmed that Cheatwood had a weapon made of wood and leather that he called his "N— beater." A hotel clerk testified that Cheatwood had bragged that he'd beaten Lyons for six or seven hours.

Marshall's argument was that the only evidence of Lyons's guilt were the two confessions he had signed, but the confessions were obtained by force, so they should be disregarded. Marshall—and everyone in the courthouse—knew that without the two confessions, there would be no evidence linking Lyons to the murder. The prosecution's case would then fall apart.

The final sentence of Section 2 of the Fourteenth Amendment requires that states provide all citizens with equal protection under the law and due process:

> *nor shall any state deprive any person of life, liberty, or property, without due process of law; nor deny to any person within its jurisdiction the equal protection of the laws.*

Due process refers to the rights of citizens to receive fair treatment under the laws and through the courts.

Marshall argued that forced confessions violated the due process clause of the Fourteenth Amendment.

The judge threw out the first confession, the one Lyons had signed after being beaten. But he allowed the second confession, the one Lyons had signed at the penitentiary, to stand. Based on the second confession, the jury found Lyons guilty. The jury, though, sentenced Lyons to life in prison instead of the death penalty. Marshall understood that if an all-white jury reduced the sentence of an African American man to life in prison, "it clearly shows that the jury believed him innocent." He added, "I think we are in a perfect position to appeal."

Shortly after the trial, the father of the murdered woman—disgusted by what he saw in the courtroom—went public with his belief that Lyons was innocent and had been framed by the police. The man's name was E. O. Colclasure. He was white, and he joined the NAACP.

★ ★ ★ ★ ★ ★ ★ ★ ★ ★ ★ ★ ★ ★ ★

While Lyons's appeal was making its way through the courts, Marshall was called to help with another police brutality case. The beatings had occurred six years earlier in Florida. Four African American men—Isiah Chambers, Jack Williamson, Charlie Davis, and Walter Woodward—had been arrested on charges of murder. They were taken to Miami for questioning. After they denied committing the murder, they were questioned under brutal circumstances: They were not permitted to sleep, they were threatened with beatings, and they were subjected to repeated and persistent questioning that went on continuously for days and nights. One officer testified that the men were questioned continually for a full week.

Justices at the Bench in the Supreme Court; one of the justices is absent.

They were at no time permitted to talk to a lawyer, a friend, or a family member. At last, each of them broke down and confessed.

Their lawyers had spent six years defending them and keeping them from being hanged while they appealed on the grounds that confessions given under such circumstances were invalid because they didn't comport with due process.

When the United States Supreme Court agreed to hear the case, Thurgood Marshall and Leon Ransom, one of his former Howard Law School professors, took over. Marshall and Ransom did the legal research and wrote the court briefs. Ransom argued in court. Their argument was straightforward: Coerced confessions violated the Fourteenth Amendment right to due process.

The Supreme Court ruled in favor of the African American defendants, holding that allowing people to be convicted based on confessions given under such circumstances would make the "constitutional requirement of due process of law a meaningless symbol." The case was styled *Chambers v. Florida* after the first named defendant. The *New York Times* declared the victory "far and away the most direct, sweeping, and brilliantly written application of the Fourteenth Amendment to human rights that has come from our highest Court."

★ ★ ★ ★ ★ ★ ★ ★ ★ ★ ★ ★ ★ ★ ★

The Supreme Court then agreed to hear Lyons's appeal. Marshall was confident they would win. After all, the men from Florida had been questioned under horrible conditions and *threatened* with beatings. Lyons had actually been beaten and tortured, which surely made his case stronger. Major newspapers began running stories about how common it was in the 1930s for African Americans to be subjected to brutal beatings at the hands of police.

This time Marshall argued the case himself. He was a seasoned debater and by then an experienced litigator. His argument was that, based on the Court's earlier ruling in *Chambers v. Florida*, both of Lyons's confessions were coerced and therefore inadmissible in court.

✴   ✴   ✴   ✴   ✴   ✴   ✴   ✴   ✴   ✴   ✴   ✴   ✴   ✴   ✴

O n June 5, 1944, the Supreme Court handed down its decision. A majority of the justices found that the second confession was valid because it was given on a different day, in a different place, and with different people present. Marshall—and Lyons—lost.

Ordinarily Marshall was respectful of rule of law and reverent toward courts. When he disagreed, he did so respectfully. But this time, in a rare outburst of fury, he told reporters that the Supreme Court's ruling gave police permission to beat a confession out of a prisoner and "then procure another before the effects of the coercion can fairly be said to have completely worn off."

7

Mr. Civil Rights

"Racism separates, but it never liberates. Hatred generates fear, and fear, once given a foothold, binds, consumes, and imprisons. Nothing is gained from prejudice. No one benefits from racism."

—Thurgood Marshall

Thurgood Marshall was by this time a national celebrity and a civil rights legend. "Thurgood's coming," for African American communities, meant that someone would fight for their rights. Herbert Hill, an NAACP official, reported that when Marshall appeared in a southern courthouse, "folks would come for miles, some of them on muleback or horseback, to see the 'N— lawyer' who stood up in white men's courtrooms."

He was in demand as a speaker. When he spoke, lecture halls

were packed. He told audiences that to achieve equality, "we need to feel in our own minds that we are the equal to anybody on the face of the globe. Anybody." With typical modesty, he gave the credit for the NAACP successes to the cadre of lawyers he'd cultivated as advisors, people like his former professors and classmates who were spread far and wide but always available to offer advice or help. "I never hesitated to pick other people's brains—brains I didn't have," he said.

One of his most harrowing experiences was in Tennessee in 1946. He had been summoned to defend twenty-five African Americans charged with assault and attempted murder. The whole thing began with a disagreement over a broken radio in a store. The store clerk tried to cheat an African American woman, Gladys Stephenson. They quarreled. The store clerk was about to hit the woman when her son James Stephenson—a World War II navy vet and former boxer—stepped between the clerk and his mother. As the mother and her son were leaving the store, the clerk—furious—hit the young man in the back of the head. In the fight that ensued, the son and the store clerk ended up on the sidewalk. Whites in the street ran up and helped beat up the African American man. The mother, frantic, stood by screaming.

Both the woman and her son were arrested and jailed. A

lynch mob gathered outside the jail but was unable to get to the mother and son, so the mob converged on an African American neighborhood called Mink Slide. African American residents of Mink Slide armed themselves and stood guard against the mob. What was later called a race riot erupted. The whites retreated and called in the Tennessee National Guard. Twenty-five African American men were arrested and charged with attempted murder.

The local NAACP lawyers managed to get the charges against James Stephenson and his mother Gladys dropped. They also persuaded an all-white jury to find twenty-three of the other men not guilty.

The two remaining accused men were found to be entitled to a new trial because of errors. Thurgood Marshall was summoned

The way NAACP lawyers could win a case in Tennessee with an all-white jury was through the process of jury selection. Defense lawyers are permitted to ask questions of perspective jurors such as "Are you a member of the KKK," or "Do you think a black man can be found innocent in a case like this?" It usually wasn't hard to uncover the to handle the second trial. He secured a verdict of not guilty for one of them. Thus only one man was found guilty.

Marshall and two other NAACP lawyers left town as soon as court adjourned. They were heading to Nashville when they realized they were being followed by a patrol car. The officers turned on the siren and motioned the terrified lawyers to the side of the road. Two police officers approached them with their guns out. The officers said they'd been tipped off that the lawyers were carrying alcohol.

The officers searched the car. They found nothing and allowed the lawyers to drive on. Before the lawyers reached Nashville, though, the officers stopped them again. This time one of the officers checked Marshall's driver's license and let him drive off.

kinds of biases that meant a juror could not be objective. No communities are entirely monolithic. Even the communities most entrenched in white supremacy had members who disagreed with the majority. Skillful lawyers make sure they dismiss jurors with obvious biases against their clients and find the ones likely to be fair.

Marshall got into the back seat and let another of the lawyers drive. They were stopped a third time. One of the officers ordered the driver out of the car. Another officer pointed to Marshall in the back seat and said, "He's the one we want." To Marshall, he said, "You're under arrest."

"What for?" Marshall asked.

"Drunk driving," the officer said.

The officer ordered Marshall into the patrol car. They turned around and sped back toward Columbia. The other two lawyers followed close behind. At one point the patrol car careened onto a side road and toward a river. Marshall had no doubt that the officer planned to kill him. When the officer realized the other lawyers were driving behind them, he pulled back onto the main highway. The patrol car pulled to a stop in front of the magistrate's office in Columbia. One officer told Marshall to walk across the street to the magistrate's office. Marshall refused. "You're not going to shoot me in the back while I'm 'escaping,'" he told them. "I mean, let's make this legal."

The officer called him a "smart-a— N—." Together they went inside to see the magistrate, a small man who stood about five feet all. The magistrate asked, "What's up?"

One of the officers said, "It's drunk driving."

"He doesn't look drunk to me," said the magistrate.

Marshall said, "I'm not drunk."

"You want to take my test?" the magistrate asked him.

"Well," Marshall said, "what's your test?"

The magistrate told Marshall he could "smell liquor a mile off." The test was for Marshall to blow his breath on the magistrate.

"Sure," Marshall said, and blew hard. Later, when telling the story, Marshall said, "I almost rocked this man, I blew so hard."

The magistrate said, "This man hasn't had a drink. What are you talking about?" He told Marshall he was free to go. Marshall met up with his two colleagues, and they went to Mink Slide for protection. To get the lawyers safely out of town, the residents of Mink Slide came up with a plan: They traded cars with the lawyers. Marshall and his two colleagues reached Nashville safely.

✶ ✶ ✶ ✶ ✶ ✶ ✶ ✶ ✶ ✶ ✶ ✶ ✶ ✶ ✶

The press began referring to Marshall as Mr. Civil Rights. Reporters photographed him getting on and off trains and airplanes. He usually wore a fedora and long tweed coat and carried a briefcase. He often stopped to scribble his phone number and hand it to someone who might need his help. He took calls from everyone. He worked nonstop.

One day he was playing cards with some friends in Washington, D.C., when he was called to the phone. The caller told him an African American man was in trouble and was about to be lynched. Marshall knew a politician from the state in question who was just then in the middle of a political campaign. Marshall tracked down his phone number and called him. "Look," he said, "just two sets of people can't afford a lynching at this time—us Negroes and you . . . a lynching's going to make your people look awful bad." The politician dashed to the scene. Twenty minutes later Marshall's phone rang again. "The state troopers made it in time," the politician said. "Call this number in a few minutes. Your man will be there, unharmed." Marshall called the number. After he was able to verify the man's safety, he returned to his card game.

★ ★ ★ ★ ★ ★ ★ ★ ★ ★ ★ ★ ★ ★ ★

Marshall's father died at home of a heart attack on March 3, 1947 at the age of sixty-six. He'd been sick for some time, and for the last years of his life worked only sporadically. The funeral was a large one. The entire extended family attended. He was buried at Arbutus Cemetery in Baltimore.

✹ ✹ ✹ ✹ ✹ ✹ ✹ ✹ ✹ ✹ ✹ ✹ ✹ ✹ ✹

Buster found a better apartment, a two-bedroom at 409 Edgecomb Avenue in Harlem. Marshall learned that one of his college buddies, Monroe Dowling, lived in their new neighborhood. Soon Dowling's wife, Helen, and Buster struck up a friendship, and the two couples often socialized in the evenings. Dowling and Marshall often got into raucous arguments. Dowling called Marshall out when he embellished stories. "Thurgood, you know d— good and well that's a lie." Marshall would laugh it off.

By this time Marshall and Buster had entirely given up hope of becoming parents. Because Marshall spent so much time on the road, their relationship became more distant. They lived almost separate lives. Buster was regularly seen at Harlem social events dancing with other men. Nobody accused her of having love affairs though; during her nights on the town, she was always in groups with friends.

The stories made Marshall jealous, but he had no room to criticize. He himself often entertained other women while on the road. He was known as a man who worked hard and played hard, and for Marshall, playing meant parties, drinking, and dancing. One of the nation's leading magazines, *Collier's*, dubbed Marshall "our greatest civil liberties lawyer," adding that he was "equally at home on a dance floor or before the U.S. Supreme Court."

Buster, of course, heard the rumors about Marshall and other women, but, according to her cousin, she didn't "make a big fuss about it." She knew he was often in danger on the road. She was more worried that he'd be murdered by an angry mob or the Ku Klux Klan than that he'd fall in love with another woman.

★ ★ ★ ★ ★ ★ ★ ★ ★ ★ ★ ★ ★ ★ ★

Meanwhile, Aubrey was still suffering from tuberculosis. His doctors advised him to get an operation on one of his lungs. Norma asked Marshall if he could find a hospital in New York that would admit Aubrey. Marshall was able to get his brother into Bellevue, where he underwent surgery. Norma came to visit Aubrey in the hospital. Thurgood and Buster spent their evenings there as well. After recovering from the operation, Aubrey was moved back to Baltimore. He regained strength, and his doctors predicted he would live.

★ ★ ★ ★ ★ ★ ★ ★ ★ ★ ★ ★ ★ ★ ★

On July 16, 1944, Irene Morgan, a civil rights activist, bought a Greyhound bus ticket from the colored window at Haye's Grocery Store in Gloucester County, Virginia. She was heading home to Baltimore. She dutifully took a seat in the colored section. She had been feeling ill, so she was happy to have found a seat with a window. Next to her was a mother with a baby.

About an hour into the trip, the bus made a stop, and a white couple boarded. The driver ordered Morgan and the mother next to her to give up their seats for the white couple. Morgan refused and encouraged the mother to do the same.

The bus driver pulled into the nearest town, Saluda, Virginia. The driver fetched an officer, who came to arrest Morgan. When the officer tried to drag her off the bus, she kicked him in the groin. She was charged with resisting arrest and violating Virginia's Jim Crow transit laws. She pleaded guilty to resisting arrest but refused to plead guilty to violating the Jim Crow laws.

She contacted Thurgood Marshall. He immediately saw the potential in the case and agreed to represent her. Her case went all the way to the United States Supreme Court, where Marshall

Irene Morgan

113

and William Hastie argued that segregation on that particular bus was illegal because it was an interstate bus and therefore beyond the reach of Virginia state laws.

> Article I of the Constitution—the article that defines the scope of the power of Congress—contains what is known as the Commerce Clause, giving Congress the power to "regulate commerce with foreign states, and among the several states . . ." The Commerce Clause has long been interpreted to mean that businesses that operate across state lines fall under federal Congressional power.

Because Morgan was on an interstate bus, Marshall and Hastie argued that the bus was subject to United States federal law, and the U.S. Congress had never enacted segregation laws—so she couldn't have been breaking any laws. They also argued that segregation on buses violated the equal protection of the Fourteenth Amendment since Morgan had not been offered equal facilities. Because they were also trying to educate the Supreme Court about the evils of segregation, Marshall and Hastie included the fact that African American soldiers had fought in large numbers in World War II to end the tyranny of Adolf Hitler and the Nazi regime—a regime steeped in racism. Even so, African Americans were still subject to racism and hate at home.

The Supreme Court agreed with Marshall and Hastie about their Commerce Clause argument. In a 7–1 vote (one of the justices was absent), the Supreme Court held that the federal government had jurisdiction over the bus under the Commerce Clause of the United States Constitution. Because no segregation laws were in place, Morgan was not guilty of lawbreaking. The Court didn't address the issue of whether segregation on interstate buses also violated the Fourteenth Amendment.

It was an astonishing victory. The ruling was hard to enforce, so interstate buses, particularly in the South, continued to segregate African Americans, but Marshall and the entire NAACP legal team basked in their success.

✶ ✶ ✶ ✶ ✶ ✶ ✶ ✶ ✶ ✶ ✶ ✶ ✶ ✶ ✶

When Marshall returned home after a court victory, Buster would invite friends over to celebrate. She'd cook his favorite dishes: pot roast, yams, and collard greens.

One of Thurgood's aunts later recalled, "Thurgood's wonderful to behold when he comes back from a hard case . . . There he is, singing—though he can't carry a tune any more than an alligator—dancing, telling funny jokes. Everyone just says, 'This is Thurgood's night; look at him go.'"

Perhaps to ease his guilt about how much he neglected his marriage, Marshall often returned from his lengthy travels with presents for Buster: pearls, a fur coat, pretty dresses, and other gifts.

★ ★ ★ ★ ★ ★ ★ ★ ★ ★ ★ ★ ★ ★ ★

Meanwhile, the equalization strategy in schools was paying off. In Virginia alone, Marshall's former classmate Oliver Hill had filed lawsuits all over the state attacking unequal facilities. Hill followed Marshall's lead, first filing suits demanding equal pay for African American teachers, then filing suits showing that the school facilities were unequal. They won court orders against the school districts, but the school boards and local communities insisted they could not obey the orders because they were short of funds.

One day Spottswood Robinson, an NAACP lawyer, was in Cumberland County, Virginia, trying to get the school district to replace tar paper shack classrooms for African American children, when a school board official said, "We'd like to help you fellas, but you're pushing too fast, and we just don't have enough money." Mr. Robinson said, "Look, I know how you could do it overnight—all you have to do is let the colored kids into Cumberland High School." A school board member then jumped to his feet and shouted, "The first little black son of a b— that comes down the road to set foot in that school, I'll take my shotgun and blow his brains out."

Oliver Hill and Spottswood Robinson, 1948

Despite widespread resistance to integration, the NAACP's widely publicized cases gave courage to African American communities. In Clarendon County, South Carolina, a gutsy teacher, Reverend Joseph Albert DeLaine, singlehandedly took on the all-white school board. The white students had a school bus. The African American students didn't. Some African American children had to ford a river and walk nine miles to the schoolhouse. When one child nearly drowned trying to cross the river to get to school, DeLaine asked the school board for a bus for the African American children. The chairman of the school board said, "We ain't got no money to buy a bus for your N— children."

There was money, though, to buy a bus for the white children. So DeLaine asked the NAACP to help him get a school bus. Thurgood Marshall told DeLaine that they would take the case if he could find twenty parents willing to sue to equalize all facilities: school buildings, books, teachers' salaries, etc.

It took DeLaine eight months to persuade twenty parents to sign up to be plaintiffs. An NAACP lawyer, Robert Carter, paid a visit to South Carolina to make sure the plaintiffs understood the danger. They did. So the NAACP filed the suit in federal court, demanding equal facilities for the African American students of Clarendon County.

The lawsuit created an uproar. Angry whites burned DeLaine's house to the ground while the Clarendon County fire department stood by and watched. DeLaine was fired from his teaching position. His wife, two sisters, and niece were also fired from their jobs. The church where he preached was set on fire. While his church was burning, he shot back at the arsonists. He didn't injure anyone, but he was charged with felonious assault with a deadly weapon. DeLaine left the state and became a fugitive.

Furious Clarendon County whites also went after the plaintiffs. Harry Briggs, the lead plaintiff, was fired from his job as a gas station attendant. Another plaintiff had his loans called in by the local bank. A small farmer needs loans to survive. Because he didn't have the money to rent harvest machinery, many of his crops rotted in the fields.

Marshall himself traveled to South Carolina and begged the residents of Clarendon County not to give up. The African American community was determined, so the lawsuit against Clarendon County moved forward. The trial was set for May, 1951, in Charleston, South Carolina.

While the Clarendon County case was working its way through the courts, Marshall was called back to Texas. Lulu

White, the director of the Texas offices of the NAACP branch, had recently given a stirring sermon pleading for someone to stand up and challenge the segregation policies of the University of Texas School of Law. Heman Sweatt, a thirty-three-year-old graduate of Wiley College in Marshall, Texas, stood up. His voice was trembling when he said he was willing to go through with it.

Heman Sweatt

So Sweatt applied for admission to the University of Texas School of Law. When he was denied admission because of his race, the NAACP filed his lawsuit against the university. The presiding judge gave the state six months to establish an education institution for African Americans. Texas rapidly created a law school at Texas State University for Negroes.

At the end of six months, Texas had a law school for African Americans. It had five professors, a library of 16,500 books, and a practice court. The University of Texas School of Law for whites had sixteen full-time professors and a library of 65,000 books.

When the case went back to court, Marshall highlighted the differences between the two schools. He also brought in law professors from around the country to testify that the new law school for African Americans could not possibly provide the same education as the all-white law school. Part of the experience of attending law school is the chance to meet future lawyers, professors who also practice law, and to become acquainted with the legal community in the state. This, of course, was not possible for students in the law school for African Americans.

Marshall also brought Donald Murray from Maryland to testify about his experiences as an African American student in an all-white law school to demonstrate to the court that no great harm would come from ordering the University of Texas to admit an African American student. The most dramatic moment in the trial came when Sweatt testified that he would not go to a segregated law school because any segregated law school was inherently unequal.

The eleven years since Marshall had filed his lawsuit for Donald Murray against the University of Maryland School of Law had brought changes. White students from the University of Texas crowded into the courtroom to hear the arguments — but this time, one white student planted himself in the colored section of the court. A court bailiff told him to move. He refused unless an African American person told him to get out. By the end of the trial—which lasted a full week—African Americans and whites were seated together all over the courtroom.

The judge presiding over the case, Roy Archer, obviously had different feelings about the matter. He told the lawyer defending Texas against the NAACP suit, "Sweatt's got two chances: slim and none."

The NAACP lost. The court ruled that the two schools provided substantially equal educations. Marshall appealed to a higher court in Texas and lost again. The Texas appellate court said that the separate-but-equal standard was satisfied by the all–African American law school.

When President Franklin D. Roosevelt died in office in 1945, his vice president, Harry S. Truman, was sworn in as president. Truman was willing to go further than Roosevelt had dared in advancing civil rights because the country was starting to shift in favor of racial equality, and in part because Harry Truman was the type to do what he thought best without worrying about losing

Marshall and his legal team immediately began working on their appeal to the United States Supreme Court. Charles Houston offered advice on the documents. Houston also contacted people he knew in the Department of Justice (DOJ), housed in Washington, D.C.

Houston persuaded the attorney general, Tom Clark, to file a brief supporting Sweatt. Clark, a progressive appointed by President Harry S. Truman, did so and argued that segregated law schools were part of a pattern that harmed African American students. The brief thus submitted by the attorney general actually asked that the "separate but equal" doctrine be overturned.

Marshall and Houston, however, were careful not to go that far. They'd been studying each of the justices and their views,

support. So in 1946, Truman established the President's Committee on Civil Rights. He also appointed Tom Clark, a native of Texas, to the post of Attorney General of the United States. As Attorney General, Clark presided over the DOJ. Clark—whom Truman later appointed to the United States Supreme Court—became a strong advocate for racial equality.

and they knew they didn't have a majority to overturn *Plessy v. Ferguson.* The last thing they wanted was for the Supreme Court to affirm the ruling in *Plessy v. Ferguson,* which would make it harder to overturn later. They simply asked for Sweatt to be admitted to the University of Texas on the grounds that a separate law school could not provide Sweatt with a legal education equivalent to what he would receive at the University of Texas School of Law.

Daniel Price, the attorney general of Texas who defended the university's segregation policies, understood very well what the NAACP was really after. Price told the justices of the Supreme Court that if the University of Texas School of Law was forced to admit Sweatt, African Americans would have to be admitted to public swimming pools, elementary schools, and hospitals. "All we ask in the South," he said, "is the opportunity to take care of this matter and work it out [ourselves]."

★ ★ ★ ★ ★ ★ ★ ★ ★ ★ ★ ★ ★ ★

While everyone was awaiting a decision from the Supreme Court on Sweatt's case, Charles Houston died of heart failure. Marshall, the NAACP, and the entire African American legal community was in shock and mourning.

Marshall told newspaper reporters who were writing about Houston that "Whatever credit is given him is not enough."

✶ ✶ ✶ ✶ ✶ ✶ ✶ ✶ ✶ ✶ ✶ ✶ ✶ ✶ ✶

The United States Supreme Court handed down its decision in Sweatt's case against the University of Texas on June 5, 1950. In a case styled *Sweatt v. Painter*, the United States Supreme Court held that the new segregated law school did not provide education equal to the more established University of Texas School of Law. The Supreme Court therefore ordered the University of Texas School of Law to admit Heman Sweatt.

The NAACP headquarters in New York erupted in celebration. Marshall, jubilant, called Sweatt to tell him the news. "We won the big one," he said.

The case was a major step forward: Under this ruling, it was basically impossible for a segregated graduate school, law school, or medical school to provide an education equal to the more established white school. The same would surely hold true for colleges and in fact *any* school.

Marshall knew the time had come to realize Charles Houston's long-cherished dream. It was time to put decades of work on the line and go after *Plessy v. Ferguson*—but still he worried about whether the time was right. Four of the Supreme Court justices were liberal-leaning, and Marshall felt they were ready to outlaw segregation. But four were more conservative, and the chief justice, Fred Vinson, was known as a weak leader. Marshall suspected Vinson was opposed to segregation, but Marshall feared that Vinson didn't have the pull or strength to lead the other justices to make the right decision.

But the *Sweatt* decision gave him the tools to go after segregation itself. The ruling in *Sweatt*—that a segregated law school could never be equal to a law school for whites—opened the door to a wider challenge: going after segregation itself by arguing that separate can never be equal.

8

Brown v. Board of Education

---

*"We are convinced that it is impossible
to have equality in a segregated system, no matter
how elaborate we build the Jim Crow citadel."*
—*Thurgood Marshall*

T hurgood Marshall and his legal team decided to begin their attack on *Plessy v. Ferguson* with the South Carolina case that had started out as a simple request for a school bus, even though Clarendon County was an unlikely place to demand full integration. Segregation was fully entrenched in South Carolina. Clarendon County was located less than one hundred miles from Fort Sumter, where, seventy-nine years earlier, a band of rebels had fired on federal troops and ignited the Civil War. There was no hope of budging

127

the majority of the white population. But the Clarendon County case was perfect for appeal. The facts were indisputable, the law was clear, and the plaintiffs—hardened and angry by the violence they'd suffered—were ready to go the full distance.

Oliver Hill, Marshall's former classmate, was working at his desk in the Richmond, Virginia NAACP office on Monday morning, April 21, 1951. He and another NAACP lawyer, Spotts-wood Robinson, were planning to drive to South Carolina on Wednesday.

His phone rang. The caller was a sixteen-year-old girl named Barbara Johns. She told Hill that she and her classmates had walked out of their segregated high school in Farmville, Vir-

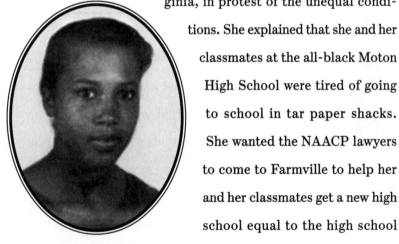

ginia, in protest of the unequal condi-tions. She explained that she and her classmates at the all-black Moton High School were tired of going to school in tar paper shacks. She wanted the NAACP lawyers to come to Farmville to help her and her classmates get a new high school equal to the high school for whites.

Barbara Johns, 1952

School bus dropping off students in front of classrooms made of tar paper

Hill told her to call off her protest and return to class. When she insisted, he told her she could write him a letter. The next day, he received a neatly typed letter signed by two students, Barbara Johns and Carrie Stokes. The youngsters explained again that they were on strike until they could get a better school. "You know that this is a very serious matter," the girls wrote, "because we are out of school, there are seniors to be graduated, and it can't be done by staying at home. Please, we beg you to come down at the first of this week . . ."

Farmville was located in Prince Edward County, Virginia. Hill figured that he and Robinson could make a detour and visit Farmville on their way to South Carolina. He contacted the local NAACP point man in Farmville, Reverend L. Francis

Griffin, and arranged to meet with the students on Wednesday
morning.

When Hill and Robinson arrived on Wednesday, they met
with the students in the basement auditorium of Reverend Griffin's church. Robinson and Hill stood in front of the group and
explained that the NAACP was no longer filing lawsuits demanding equal facilities. From then on, the NAACP would only file
lawsuits demanding full integration. If the African American
community of Farmville wanted the NAACP to file a lawsuit
for integration, the NAACP would consider it—but only if the
students' parents were solidly behind them, and only if they all
understood the dangers.

Hill and Robinson had the same opinion: Farmville was a
rural backwater. They believed it unlikely that the Farmville
parents would get behind a lawsuit for full integration. They left
that morning, believing they'd heard the last from the Moton
students.

Two weeks later, W. Lester Banks, executive secretary of the
Virginia NAACP office, reported that the Farmville students had
gotten their parents to agree to sue Prince Edward County for full
integration. Even after a cross was burned on the Moton High
School grounds, the African American community stood firm. So

on May 7, the NAACP filed a petition with the Prince Edward
school board demanding that the Moton students be admitted to
the all-white Farmville High School. As everyone expected, the
board rejected the petition. So, on Monday, May 23, 1951, the Virginia office of the NAACP filed a lawsuit in Prince Edward County
demanding full integration of the county's public schools.

In 1951, more than eleven thousand school districts
in the United States were segregated. Seventeen
states required segregation in schools. An additional
four permitted local communities to segregate their
schools.

Fourteen states required segregated railroad cars
in 1951.

Ten states required different waiting rooms for bus
and train travelers.

Eight states segregated parks, playgrounds,
bathing and fishing facilities, circuses, theaters, and
public halls.

In Alabama, a white nurse was forbidden to care
for an African American man in a hospital.

★　★　★　★　★　★　★　★　★　★　★　★　★　★

Two psychologists, Kenneth and Mamie Clark, had devised psychological tests showing that segregation harmed African American children. They conducted experiments with dark- and light-skinned dolls. The experiments were straightforward: They handed young children two dolls, a light-skinned doll and a dark-skinned doll, and asked questions like, "Hand me the doll you like best," or "Hand me the doll that looks bad." African American children throughout the nation favored the light-skinned doll.

Marshall decided to use Clark's experiments as evidence in his school desegregation cases. Initially the idea met with resistance among NAACP lawyers. Spottswood Robinson thought it was crazy and insulting to try to persuade a court of law with studies about children and dolls. But Marshall stood firm. He saw no reason not to use psychological studies if it might help the case.

The Clarendon County trial was held in May of 1951. More than five hundred people came to watch. The courtroom had a maximum capacity of seventy-five, so most stood outside, straining to hear. "They came in their jalopy cars and their overalls, and they had this little section of the court where they could go.

Brown v. Board of Education

All they wanted to do—if they could—was just touch him, just touch him, *Lawyer Marshall*, as if he were a god. These were poor people who had come miles to be there."

At the trial, Marshall called Dr. Clark as a witness and introduced his psychological studies. Marshall also brought college professors from Columbia and Harvard, who testified about the harmful effects of segregation on African American children. Clarendon County responded that if the court forced them to provide equal education for African American children, they'd go broke and would not be able to offer education to *any* children. Local whites firmly believed that because African Americans, as a group, paid fewer taxes, they were not entitled to facilities equal to the children of parents whose taxes supported the county.

The district federal judge, though, was on Marshall's side. The district court found the facilities grossly unequal and ordered Clarendon County to provide equal facilities for the African American children. The district court didn't respond to the broader question of whether segregation itself was illegal. This didn't surprise Marshall. District courts were bound to follow precedent set by the Supreme Court. Only the United States Supreme Court could overrule *Plessy v. Ferguson*.

✴ ✴ ✴ ✴ ✴ ✴ ✴ ✴ ✴ ✴ ✴ ✴ ✴ ✴ ✴

Meanwhile, the Prince Edward County plaintiffs lost their case in district court. The court found that Moton High School was equal to Farmville High School, even though Farmville High had a modern building, a gym, a cafeteria, and modern equipment. Because of overcrowding, Moton students attended class in leaky shacks made of tar paper and wood.

By the time the NAACP filed its appeals to the Supreme Court for both the South Carolina and Virginia cases, they were able to join those two cases with two other related cases from Kansas and Washington, D.C. The plaintiffs were listed alphabetically, which put the father of Kansas student Linda Brown first. The consolidated cases were called *Brown v. Board of Education.* This time the NAACP was demanding full integration and an end to *Plessy v. Ferguson.*

✴ ✴ ✴ ✴ ✴ ✴ ✴ ✴ ✴ ✴ ✴ ✴ ✴ ✴ ✴

When the Supreme Court decided to hear *Brown v. Board of Education,* criticism and anger poured in from all sides. A *Pittsburgh Courier* columnist wrote that Marshall was leading everyone over a cliff: Decisions such as *Sweatt* *v. Painter* put African Americans on a clear road to equal educations. Now he was risking it all by trying to force all communities to integrate. People predicted doom. It was unthinkable, people argued, that whites would allow African Americans to teach their students. All the African American teachers and principals would be out of a job. Marshall ignored the criticism. He kept his head down and focused on preparing his legal briefs.

Chief Justice Fred Vinson scheduled oral arguments for *Brown v. Board of Education* to begin on December 9, 1952. Marshall was so fixated on preparing for the oral arguments that he neglected everything else, including his health. He smoked, gained weight, and had trouble sleeping. He had books and papers strewn everywhere.

He called together the brightest lawyers he knew to discuss every possible angle. There were heated disagreements about the best arguments and responses. When arguments erupted, Marshall often lightened the mood by cracking a joke. "Thurgood had an incredible gift," said one of his assistants. "He'd have his feet up on the table, with all these learned minds around him, in awe of him. He'd make them feel at home. He would pull out from other people their thinking, and he synthesized it and made it his."

The law students and faculty at Howard Law School helped Marshall prepare by holding mock Supreme Court arguments. The students and faculty threw the trickiest questions they could think of at him and other members of his legal team.

Buster had not been feeling well for a while. She felt tired even after a full night's sleep, but she was more worried about Thurgood. "He's aged so much in the past five years," she said. "His disposition's changed, he's nervous where he used to be calm—this work is taking its toll of him." She added: "You know, it's a discouraging job he's set himself."

The Clarendon defendants brought John W. Davis out of retirement to argue their case for them at the Supreme Court. Davis was the lawyer whom Marshall had crept away from law school to watch in awe. Now, in the crowning case of Marshall's own career, he would face off against Davis. Marshall was forty-four years old. Davis, who was seventy-nine, had argued more cases before the United States Supreme Court than any other living person.

Davis invited Marshall to lunch before their Supreme Court appearance. Marshall accepted his invitation, shocking his friends, family, and colleagues. Davis represented everything they were working against: the genteel and well-educated southern

gentleman who took for granted that
the white race was superior and
that segregation benefitted both
races. Marshall explained that
"It's very important to have a
civil relationship with your opponent." When they met for lunch,
Davis was impeccably dressed and
unfailingly polite.

John W. Davis, circa 1922

ORDER FOR APPEARANCE

Supreme Court of the United States

No. 436 , October Term, 19

Office - Supreme Court, U. S.
RECEIVED
DEC 3 – 1951
CHARLES ELMORE CROPLEY
CLERK

BROWN, et al.

vs.

BOARD OF EDUCATION, et al.

The Clerk will enter my appearance as Counsel for the _____ Appellants

(*Name*) *Thurgood Marshall*
Thurgood Marshall

(*Address*) *20 W. 40th St*
New York (18) N.Y.

NOTE.—Must be signed by a member of the Bar of the Supreme Court United States. Individual and not firm names must be signed. Type or print name under signature.

Supreme Court order for Thurgood Marshall's appearance
as part of the *Brown v. Board of Education* case

On the morning of December 9, 1952, hundreds of people stood in line, hoping to hear the arguments. Some had been there all night. Buster was still feeling ill, but she drove to Washington to attend. When Marshall and Davis took their places at the podiums, the chamber was packed.

Marshall was shocked when Justice Frankfurter, who he thought would be sympathetic to his arguments, opened by shooting questions at him, like whether Marshall would object to a plan that segregated based on eye color. "No, sir," Marshall responded, "because blue-eyed people in the United States never had the badge of slavery which was perpetuated in the statutes." The barrage of questions, though, rattled him. Later he said, "Frankfurter was a smart aleck, you know."

John W. Davis urged the court not to overturn decades of precedent. His voice was well modulated and respectful as he insisted that the Fourteenth Amendment was never intended to intrude on the rights of local communities to manage their own educational programs. He pointed out that the local communities were complying with the order that they provide equal facilities. He dismissed the social science arguments offered by Marshall, stating that although they may be of interest to legislatures as they designed their laws, they had no place in constitutional arguments. "We shall get a finer, better balance of spirit," he said, "an infinitely more capable and rounded personality, by putting children where they are wanted and where they are happy and inspired, than in thrusting them into the hells where they are ridiculed and hated."

Each group of defendants had a chance to present arguments. Marshall had to rebut each of them. The questioning lasted five exhausting days. When the arguments concluded, Marshall went home for Christmas to recover.

✴ ✴ ✴ ✴ ✴ ✴ ✴ ✴ ✴ ✴ ✴ ✴ ✴ ✴ ✴

onths passed without a decision. Then, on June 8, 1953, the Supreme Court shocked everyone by issuing such questions to the lawyers on all sides as:

> *Did the Supreme Court have the power to abolish school*
> *segregation?*
> *Did the framers of the Fourteenth Amendment intend to*
> *end school segregation?*
> *How would integration be managed if the Court voted to*
> *mix African American and white schoolchildren?*

Preparing the answers took months and was costly. The NAACP's final brief was 256 pages. The NAACP responded to each question, offering historical and legal justification that the court could make such a ruling. Their overarching argument was that upholding school segregation made sense only if the Court concluded that African Americans were inferior to whites.

Before a second round of arguments could be scheduled, Chief Justice Fred Vinson died of a heart attack. It fell to the newly elected President Dwight D. Eisenhower to appoint a new chief justice. Eisenhower appointed former Oakland, California, prosecutor and politician Earl Warren. The appointment set off alarm bells in the NAACP. Warren had served as California attorney general and governor during World War II. When the Japanese had attacked the United States at Pearl Harbor, people of Japanese descent living on the West Coast had been confined in isolated camps. Warren had helped carry out the internment orders and had even advocated interning Japanese Americans.

Marshall did his own research on Warren. He went to

The internment of Japanese Americans in camps resulted from widespread fear that anyone with Japanese heritage was a potential traitor. About 120,000 people were interned, surrounded by barbed wire and armed guards. They lost

California to learn everything he could. Both liberals and conservatives he spoke to said the same thing: The man was great. Two California judges assured Marshall that Warren would do the right thing, whatever he felt it was. People told Marshall that Warren was a man of integrity. He was independent. He did what he thought was best, and he didn't like racial segregation. Marshall concluded that the internment of the Japanese did not reflect Warren's current thinking about race in America. He came to believe that he could count on Warren's vote. If his calculations were correct, he was thus assured of the votes of five of the nine justices, which would be a win.

Earl Warren, 1953

their homes and jobs, even though there was no evidence that they'd done anything wrong. Later, when Warren wrote his memoirs, he expressed deep remorse and guilt for the part he played in the internment of the Japanese.

The second round of arguments was scheduled for December 8, 1953. Again, Marshall plunged into months of preparation and study. This time he had to be ready to talk on a new range of issues—the contents of the briefs submitted by all four counties and his own 256-page brief.

Buster, meanwhile, was feeling ill more often. Some mornings she couldn't rise from her bed. She underwent a battery of medical tests. She minimized her illness to Marshall. She was afraid

From left to right, Harold R. Boulware, Thurgood Marshall, and Spottswood W. Robinson confer before the Supreme Court argument in *Brown v. Board of Education.*

that if she revealed to him how sick she was, he'd be distracted from his work and his mission. When her illness worsened, her parents came to stay and care for her.

The oral arguments for *Brown v. Board of Education* began on December 8, 1953 and continued for two days. Again the courtroom was packed. Marshall's mother, Norma, sat with Buster in the reserved section.

On the first day, Marshall felt his performance was subpar, even though he ended on a strong note, telling the court that segregation sprang from a desire "to keep people who were formerly in slavery . . . as near that stage as is possible."

The second day, Marshall found his footing. He "came on like a locomotive," said one of the Kansas lawyers. He easily rebutted the arguments made by Davis and the other school board lawyers that bringing children of different races together in a classroom would be somehow harmful. "These same kids in Virginia and South Carolina—and I have seen them do it—they play together in the streets, they play on their farms together, they go down the road together, they separate to go to school, they come out of the school and play ball together."

At 2:00 p.m. on December 10, after the closing remarks, the court adjourned.

★ ✷ ✷ ✷ ✷ ✷ ✷ ✷ ✷ ✷ ✷ ✷ ✷ ✷ ✷

O n Sunday, May 16, 1954, Marshall was in Mobile, Alabama on a speaking tour to raise money for the Legal Defense Fund. He was expected in Los Angeles the following morning.

He received a phone call. Later, he refused to name the caller. The person told him that he might want to be at the Supreme Court the following day. Marshall cancelled his event in Los Angeles and caught the next flight to Washington, D.C.

✷ ✷ ✷ ✷ ✷ ✷ ✷ ✷ ✷ ✷ ✷ ✷ ✷ ✷ ✷

M arshall and his legal team sat in the formal chambers facing the nine Supreme Court justices. The justices were prepared to issue their decision in *Brown v. Board of Education*. The chamber was crowded and crackled with tension.

Chief Justice Earl Warren began to speak. First he outlined the basic facts of the cases, then he reviewed the legal questions. Finally he said, "We conclude that in the field of public education, the doctrine of 'separate but equal' has no place. Separate educational facilities are inherently unequal."

They'd won! "I was so happy I was numb," Marshall said later.

A woman named Nettie Hunt, on the Supreme Court steps, explains what the headline "High Court Bans Segregation in Schools" means to her daughter.

The biggest surprise: The decision was unanimous. Marshall learned later that Earl Warren had spent months working to bring all nine justices together, which was why the decision had taken so long.

The moment the justices filed out of the courtroom, Marshall was mobbed by reporters. His first words were, "We hit the jackpot." There was one child in the courtroom, the son of Joe Greenhill, an assistant attorney general from Texas who had argued against Marshall in the Sweatt case. Greenhill was on vacation and had his family with him. As Greenhill later described, Marshall "picked up our son Bill and put him on his shoulders and ran down the corridor of the Supreme Court . . . He was having a good time, and we were having a good time. To h— with dignity. He just won a biggie."

★ ★ ★ ★ ★ ★ ★ ★ ★ ★ ★ ★ ★ ★

Many years later, when speaking about the decision in *Brown v. Board of Education*, Chief Justice Earl Warren said, "I don't remember having any great doubts about which way it should go. It seemed to me a comparatively simple case. Just look at the various decisions that had been eroding *Plessy* for so many years." Initially two justices had held out, with seven in favor of ending segregation. The only hard part for Warren had been getting a forceful enough decision from a unanimous Court to make sure they put an end to Jim Crow once and for all.

9

Massive Resistance

"What is striking is the role legal principles have played throughout America's history in determining the condition of Negroes. They were enslaved by law, emancipated by law, disenfranchised and segregated by law; and, finally, they have begun to win equality by law."

— Thurgood Marshall

The furious backlash began immediately. "The South will not abide by or obey this legislative decision by the Court," said Mississippi Senator James Eastland. Richard Russell, a senator from Georgia, accused the Supreme Court of striking down "the rights of the states, as guaranteed by the Constitution, to direct their most vital local affairs." Governor Herman Talmadge of Georgia said racial integration was the "first step toward national suicide." U.S. Senator Harry F. Byrd of Virginia declared that his state was undertaking what he called a massive resistance.

President Eisenhower privately fumed. The task of enforcing the *Brown v. Board of Education* decision would fall to the executive branch, and he deeply resented being put in such a position. "I personally think the decision was wrong," he told a staffer.

In November 1954, while Marshall was scrambling to deal with school boards refusing to desegregate, Buster was diagnosed with lung cancer. She told Marshall by telephone. She also told him that she wasn't expected to live much longer. He rushed home, shocked to find out he was among the last to learn how sick she was. She wanted to return to her childhood home in Philadelphia. He stopped work completely to go with her. For the next three months, he was by her side constantly, caring for her himself. In January, she told a reporter, "If I had my life to live over again, I wouldn't change any part of it. I have wanted most, all these years, to help [Thurgood] make good."

Vivian Burey Marshall died February 11, 1955, on her forty-fourth birthday. She and Marshall had been married for twenty-five years. Marshall sank into a depression. "During this time," said an NAACP lawyer, "he lost so much weight that he became cadaverous in appearance." He didn't have the heart to work, so he went on an extended vacation to Mexico. While he was gone, Walter White died, and the talk was that Marshall should take over his position as executive director of the NAACP—but Marshall was unable to think about working. "He took her death very, very hard," said Alice Stovall, Marshall's secretary.

After two months in Mexico, he returned to New York. In April, he went back to work. With school districts refusing to integrate, there was much work to be done. Once more, the battles would have to be fought in the courts.

As the nation's most famous and accomplished African American man, Marshall suddenly found himself talked about as a very eligible bachelor. Women began stopping by the NAACP offices, hoping to catch his eye. Harlem gossips speculated on what lay in his romantic future. Marshall ignored the chatter. He had court appearances to prepare for, briefs to write, meetings to attend, and speeches to deliver.

✳ ✳ ✳ ✳ ✳ ✳ ✳ ✳ ✳ ✳ ✳ ✳ ✳ ✳ ✳

In November 1955—one year after Buster told Marshall she was dying and nine months after her death—Marshall concluded a secret, whirlwind courtship by proposing marriage to Cecilia "Cissy" Suyat, a secretary at the NAACP. Cissy had been born in Hawaii to parents who immigrated from the Philippines. She had moved to New York as a young woman and landed a job at the NAACP, which she saw as a "blessing . . . maybe my guardian angels were watching over me." In Hawaii she'd lived in a culturally diverse neighborhood and never experienced discrimination because she was a Filipina. At the NAACP her eyes were opened to the problem of racial discrimination. She started working as a stenographer and was later promoted to secretary. She was the secretary who had taken the lawyers' notes as they prepared for the Supreme Court arguments in *Brown v. Board of Education.*

She was petite, less than five feet tall. Marshall was six feet two. He would say, "How's the weather down there, gal?" and she would answer, "Same as up there, man!" She liked to add, "I don't care how tall you are. I can still beat you up. I'll get on a chair."

Not long after Marshall and Cissy announced their engagement, a political activist named Rosa Parks refused to give up her seat on a Montgomery bus to a white man. Parks was arrested and charged with violating the city's bus ordinances. Marshall received a phone call from E. D. Nixon, a colleague at the Montgomery, Alabama, branch of the NAACP. Nixon asked Marshall to represent a group that was planning to boycott the city's segregated buses. Nixon anticipated that the boycott would last about a day. Marshall agreed to offer the group legal representation.

Rosa Parks is arrested.

Meanwhile, Marshall and Cissy decided to get married right away. Cissy was twenty-six years old, and Marshall was forty-six. Marshall wanted children. They were married on December 17, 1955. After the wedding, Cissy resigned from her job at the NAACP and became a homemaker.

The newlyweds left for a two-week honeymoon in the Caribbean. When they returned in January, Marshall was stunned to learn that the Montgomery Bus Boycott was still going on—and that it was grabbing headlines all over the country. "We were advising them of the legal steps to be made. We were proceeding when all of a sudden this preacher started jumping out of there. We'd never heard of him before. I knew his father in Atlanta, but I'd never heard of him until then."

The preacher—a brilliant and mesmerizing speaker—was Rev. Martin Luther King Jr. He was then twenty-seven years old. At first he had been hesitant about taking a leading role in the bus boycott. Then he threw himself entirely into a leadership role. When he spoke, he stirred crowds to action. "We are tired," he said, "tired of being segregated and humiliated, tired of being kicked around by the brutal feet of oppression."

When the boycott grew into an actual movement, Thurgood Marshall had deep reservations. He didn't think protests were the way to win rights. After years of seeing demonstrations and riots turn violent, he was afraid of stirring unrest. Ironically, Thurgood Marshall and the NAACP were blamed for fomenting trouble when in fact they had no control over the outpouring of protesters. The *New Yorker* identified Thurgood

Marshall as the ringleader and mastermind behind the boycott, an accusation that amused him and which he vehemently denied.

Marshall and Martin Luther King Jr. got to know each other. While they agreed about much, they disagreed over the idea of civil disobedience.

Civil disobedience, or passive resistance, means refusing to obey unjust laws. People engaging in civil disobedience understand that they are subject to punishment, but they hope to set a moral example and show that the laws are unjust. The modern concept of civil disobedience was most clearly articulated by Mahatma Gandhi, an Indian lawyer who became a leader against British rule in India. Later the concept was adopted by many of the American civil rights leaders, most notably Martin Luther King Jr.

"I used to have a lot of fights with Martin about his theory about disobeying the law," Marshall said later. "I didn't believe in that. I thought you did have a right to disobey a law, and you also had a right to go to jail for it." Marshall wanted people to work within the law.

Despite his inward reservations, Marshall outwardly supported the boycott because it was peaceful with no lawbreaking. When he appeared on *Youth Wants to Know*, a national TV program, he praised King highly for refusing to use or allow violence.

★ ★ ★ ★ ★ ★ ★ ★ ★ ★ ★ ★ ★ ★ ★

Marshall took the Montgomery Bus Boycott case to a local Montgomery court. He and his legal team relied on the precedent they'd established in two decades of case law and *Brown v. Board of Education*. They won. The court banned segregated busing in Montgomery. The city, though, refused to integrate its buses until the appeals were completed—so the boycott continued as the NAACP prepared its appeal.

★ ★ ★ ★ ★ ★ ★ ★ ★ ★ ★ ★ ★ ★ ★

Meanwhile, a young woman named Autherine Lucy, twenty-seven years old, wanted to enroll in the University of Alabama. She had applied in 1952 and was accepted, but the university withdrew her acceptance when they learned she was African American. In 1955, the NAACP took her case to court, where a federal judge ordered the University of Alabama to admit her. When she arrived on campus for the first day of class, an angry mob gathered and threatened her life. The mob grew even angrier. Fearing for her life, she locked herself in a room until she could be rescued by state police. The school then barred Lucy from attending on the grounds that attending the University of Alabama would be unsafe for her.

Thurgood Marshall and NAACP official Roy Wilkins in a press conference with Autherine Lucy, 1956

Marshall was in the Birmingham home of NAACP lawyer Arthur Shores, preparing for a court appearance on Lucy's behalf, when a car careened onto the sidewalk. A man tried to throw a bomb toward the house, but the bomb went off in the man's hand, blowing off part of his arm. The car careened away, leaving the wounded man behind. The lawyers ran outside and applied towels to his wound until the ambulance arrived.

When NAACP lawyers accused the university officials of conspiring with the mob, the university permanently expelled Lucy from attending school on the grounds that she had slandered the university with falsehoods. The NAACP was unable to reverse her expulsion. It wasn't until 1992 that Lucy was finally able to earn a master's degree from the University of Alabama.

★ ★ ★ ★ ★ ★ ★ ★ ★ ★ ★ ★ ★ ★ ★

Thurgood Marshall's first son, Thurgood Junior, was born in 1956. Thurgood's mother, Norma, moved to New York to live with her sister, Medi, and brother-in-law, Boots. Thurgood, Cissy, and the baby often visited them. With the arrival of the baby, Marshall wanted to stay home more and travel less—but he couldn't. There was too much work for him to do. The Montgomery boycott was in its sixth month. While waiting to see if the United States Supreme Court would hear the case, the city of Montgomery sued Martin Luther King Jr. for promoting the boycott. The NAACP represented him at no cost.

On November 13, 1956, the Supreme Court rejected Alabama's appeal, allowing the lower court decision to stand. The city of Montgomery now had no choice but to allow African Americans to sit where they wished on buses. Martin Luther King Jr. was one of the first passengers to ride an integrated city bus.

Martin Luther King Jr. and civil rights activist Ralph Abernathy ride the first desegregated bus in Montgomery, Alabama.

The newspapers gave Martin Luther King Jr., Rosa Parks, and the protesters credit for desegregating Montgomery's buses. Watching, Marshall felt resentful—and exhausted. Biographer Juan Williams wrote that in Marshall's view, the boycott had been mere "street theater." The actual work had been done by the lawyers.

Years of nonstop travel and litigation was taking its toll. One of Marshall's friends told *Life Magazine* that Marshall, formerly an easygoing lawyer, had become as tense as "a teakettle about to explode."

✶　✶　✶　✶　✶　✶　✶　✶　✶　✶　✶　✶　✶　✶　✶

In August 1957, Marshall was called to Little Rock, Arkansas, for an emergency. Violence was about to erupt. The reason? Nine African American students planned to enroll in the all-white Central High School. When Marshall arrived in Little Rock, armed guards escorted him to the home of activist Daisy Bates, where he and the other lawyers handling the case would stay.

On September 2, the governor of Arkansas, Orval Eugene Faubus, ordered the National Guard to prevent African American students from entering Central High. If any African Americans tried to enter, he warned that "blood will run in the street."

Tensions were so high that at night, African Americans kept their homes dark so that they wouldn't be targets for drive-by shooters or bomb-throwers.

Orval Faubus holds a sign saying "Against racial integration . . ."

On September 3, Marshall obtained an order from a federal judge forbidding Faubus from using members of the National Guard to prevent students from entering a school. Marshall wanted President Eisenhower to step in to de-escalate the tension, but to his annoyance, Eisenhower coddled Governor Faubus. So Marshall tried to leverage public opinion by issuing a press release calling for Eisenhower to take command away from the Arkansas governor. This further enraged many whites. Guards stationed to protect Daisy Bates's house stopped a group of whites approaching with dynamite.

By the 1950s, America had entered the age of television. Prior to 1947, fewer than one thousand households owned television sets, and TV programming was viewed as nothing more than radio with pictures. In 1952, television news covered the presidential nominating conventions. The power of television as a cultural force increased in 1956, when TV created the news videotape, which gave the news immediacy and allowed viewers to feel more intimately connected to events happening far away.

On September 23—the first day of classes—the first African American student arrived. In front of the school was an angry mob who taunted her. When she tried to enter the building, the mob surrounded her and shouted, "Lynch her! Lynch her!" She was saved by a white woman who shielded her until she could run away from the school to safety. The mob grew to about a thousand people. When the other eight African American students arrived, they, too, were blocked from entering the building by angry, sneering crowds. The mob attacked reporters and African American pass-ersby. The police removed all eight youngsters and brought them to safety.

Journalists filmed foot-age of the jeering crowds and mob violence in Little Rock. The videotapes played widely on television. The raw hatred directed at

African American student Elizabeth Eckford endures verbal abuse hurled at her outside Central High School in Little Rock, Arkansas. National Guardsman in upper left of photo.

African American youth rattled the conscience of the nation.

✳ ✳ ✳ ✳ ✳ ✳ ✳ ✳ ✳ ✳ ✳ ✳ ✳ ✳ ✳

Arkansas Senator John McClellan held Thurgood Marshall responsible for the fact that, as a result of the news vid-eotapes, Little Rock was widely viewed as mean and bigoted. The mayor of Little Rock desperately wired Eisenhower, asking him to do something. Eisenhower had not wanted to be the president who sent troops to quell citizens, but at last he acted. He ordered the 101st Airborne from Fort Campbell in Kentucky to Little Rock. He also gave a nationally televised speech reminding the nation that mob rule could not be allowed to override court decisions. The next day, federal troops arrived to escort the African American students to school. The troops circled the school and chaperoned the nine young people down the corridors.

Newspaperman Mike Wallace asked Marshall if he and the NAACP had started a second Civil War. Marshall answered, "If you mean by Civil War that there is continuing effort to emancipate Negros, toward accomplishing what the Civil War was intended to accomplish—yes." In this interview, Marshall also blasted President Eisenhower for not doing more to prevent such uprisings. "The president should have, shortly after the decision, gone on television or radio and spoken as the chief executive of this government, to the good people of the South, urging them to support the ruling of the Supreme Court, which is the law of the land."

★ ★ ★ ★ ★ ★ ★ ★ ★ ★ ★ ★ ★ ★ ★

By this time, Marshall understood his mistake. After getting the ruling in *Brown* three years earlier, he and the NAACP "should have sat down and planned," because "the other side did. The other side planned all the delaying tactics they could think of." The lesson: If you are attempting to bring about a major change in the structure of the society, be ready for the backlash.

✶ ✶ ✶ ✶ ✶ ✶ ✶ ✶ ✶ ✶ ✶ ✶ ✶ ✶ ✶

The year Marshall turned fifty, 1958, Cissy gave birth to their second child, John. Marshall did his best to stay home more. He and Cissy threw parties. He tried his hand at cooking. Insiders of the New York Democratic Party, sometimes known as the party bosses, looked at him as a possible candidate for office. But he had no interest in running for office. He had been practicing law for twenty-eight years. He wanted to slow down. He wanted time with his wife and sons.

Thurgood Marshall reading to Thurgood Marshall Jr., twenty-two months old

10

Judge Marshall

"It is the responsibility of the judiciary to make sure that we remain a government of laws and that all persons are equal under those laws. That is the essence of justice."

—Thurgood Marshall

On February 1, 1960, four college students in Greensboro, North Carolina refused to leave a Woolworth's whites-only lunch counter. Their sit-in sparked similar protests throughout the country. When the students were arrested, the parents asked the NAACP to get them out of jail. Marshall didn't like it at all. The Legal Defense Fund was intended to protect innocent African Americans who had been wrongly accused, not radical youths who were intentionally breaking the law.

Marshall was then traveling in Kenya and Great Britain. He was helping the native Kenyans, who were struggling to gain independence from British colonial rule, draft their new constitution. When he returned to New York, he went to the NAACP offices to deal with the crisis.

"Thurgood stormed around the room," said one observer, "proclaiming in a voice that could be heard across Columbus Circle that he did not care what anyone said, he was not going to represent a bunch of crazy colored students . . ." If the students don't like the laws, Marshall insisted, they needed to change the laws using legal means.

His legal staff came up with a Fourteenth Amendment argument: A restaurant open to the public operated under the protection of the laws of the state; therefore, a business that barred members of the public because of their race was violating the equal protection clause of the Fourteenth Amendment. Marshall thought it over. He became a convert. He allocated money to defend the sit-in protesters on a Fourteenth Amendment equal protection argument.

NAACP opponents accused them of reading things into the Constitution that were not there. The plain language of the Fourteenth Amendment referred to *state* action: ". . . nor shall any state deprive any person of life, liberty, or property, without due process of law; nor deny any person within its jurisdiction the equal protection of the laws." It was bad enough, NAACP

The Constitution contains a great many words and phrases that are vague and morally charged. People are inclined to read into these phrases whatever ideas they have to start with. For example, does "liberty" mean restaurant owners should be free to refuse entry to African Americans on the basis of their race? Or does liberty mean that any citizen should be able to walk into any place open to the general public?

Even before the Constitution was ratified, the founders were debating how the Constitution should be interpreted.

Alexander Hamilton advocated a loose interpretation that would allow flexibility. He understood that viewing the constitution as ironclad would prevent growth and change, forever freezing the country as it stood in the eighteenth century.

Hamilton's rival, Thomas Jefferson, held the opposite view. He put forward what has been called the originalist view of the Constitution, which holds that the Constitution must

66
666
666

enemies insisted, that the courts applied the Fourteenth Amendment to schools. Applying the Fourteenth Amendment to private stores and restaurants, in their view, distorted the Constitution

be read exactly as it was intended, and any proposed change must go through the cumbersome amendment process. Jefferson believed that allowing for a loose interpretation would result in lack of stability because everyone would have a different idea of what vague words should mean.

The Warren Court (the court is always named after its chief justice) adopted a theory called *contemporary ratification*. Instead of asking "What did these words mean when they were drafted and ratified?", the theory of contemporary ratification says a court should ask, "What do these words mean in our time." Critics believed that contemporary ratification allowed the Supreme Court to invent out of whole cloth whatever rule they wanted and claim that it was based in the Constitution.

Originalism, which impedes change, is the favorite of conservatives. Contemporary ratification, which allows for change, is embraced by liberals.

and infringed on the personal liberty of restaurant and store owners.

★ ★ ★ ★ ★ ★ ★ ★ ★ ★ ★ ★ ★ ★ ★

In October 1960, Martin Luther King Jr. and several other protestors were arrested and jailed for a sit-in at Rich's Department Store in Atlanta. The NAACP lawyers immediately set to work to get King and the protestors released.

America was then in the midst of a presidential election pitting Republican Richard Nixon against Democrat John F. Kennedy. The two candidates responded differently to King's arrest. Nixon called the Justice Department to make sure King was being treated properly in jail. Kennedy called King's wife, Coretta, and promised to do what he could to get King out of jail. Robert Kennedy, the candidate's brother, contacted the judge overseeing the case and asked for King's release.

When King was released, Robert Kennedy got the credit. The NAACP lawyer, who had been working long hours to get King released from jail, felt miffed. Marshall congratulated the lawyer who had secured King's release and said, "You know, they tell me everybody in the world got Martin Luther King Jr. out but the lawyer." They all laughed.

While Robert Kennedy's phone call to the judge had not been of any legal significance, it was a savvy political move, demonstrating commitment to the cause of racial equality. The African American vote came out for Kennedy.

The election was a close one. John F. Kennedy was elected president with 49.72 percent of the vote to Nixon's 49.55.

Around this time, Norma Marshall, Thurgood's mother, grew ill. Thurgood, Cissy, and Norma's sister Medi cared for her. In August 1961, Norma Marshall died in New York. She was seventy-four. The funeral was held at St. Philip's in Harlem. It was a simple ceremony, attended by family and close friends. Aubrey, who had never fully regained his strength after his tuberculosis, came from Baltimore to attend.

✸ ✸ ✸ ✸ ✸ ✸ ✸

Thurgood Marshall, Cissy, and their two children, John (left) and Thurgood Jr., in their New York apartment

O n September 23, 1961, President Kennedy nominated Thurgood Marshall to serve as a judge on the U.S. Second Circuit Court of Appeals. Marshall wouldn't be the first African American appointed as a federal appellate judge—Bill Hastie, his former Howard law professor, had been first in 1931, followed by a handful of others.

The Constitution gives the president the power to appoint federal judges with "advice and consent" from the Senate. The senators—mostly hailing from the South—who didn't want Marshall on the federal bench resorted to delay tactics. They refused

Federal courts were created under Article III of the Constitution to "administer justice fairly and impartially." There are three levels of courts in the federal system. The lowest level is trial courts, also called district courts, which conduct trials and resolve conflicts. The second level is the courts of appeal, or appellate courts, for parties dissatisfied with lower court decisions. Appellate courts are also called circuit courts because, when the nation was young, there were no appointed judges to hear appeals. Instead, two Supreme Court justices and a trial court judge would "ride circuit," to show up for hearings. They found excuses for postponement. Ten months passed. Meanwhile, segregationist judges were quickly confirmed.

Jackie Robinson, a columnist, wrote that Marshall was being punished for the color of his skin. Former First Lady Eleanor Roosevelt threw her weight behind Marshall's appointment, calling the delay a worldwide embarrassment to a nation that professed equality among its citizens. When at last Marshall's confirmation was put to the vote, the Senate voted to confirm him as a federal judge.

traveling around the country to the various appellate courts to hear appeals and resolve them. In 1869, Congress passed the Circuit Court Act, funding at least one judge for each court of appeals, so there was no longer any need for riding circuit.

The highest court in the land is the Supreme Court. A person who is dissatisfied with the decision of an appellate court can ask the Supreme Court to hear their case. The Constitution also allows a few kinds of cases to be appealed directly to the Supreme Court, including cases in which a state is a party and cases involving foreign officials.

★ ★ ★ ★ ★ ★ ★ ★ ★ ★ ★ ★ ★ ★ ★

Being the newest member of the Second Circuit Court of Appeals meant that Marshall handled the more routine and less interesting cases. He found himself untangling the minutiae of tax law and trying to determine the meanings of obscure statutes. One friend thought he was a little bored.

The work might have been a bit dull, but the Second Circuit Court was located in New York City, so he achieved his wish of traveling less. He was also earning more money than he'd ever earned before. His sons attended good schools. His life felt more settled.

He watched now from the sidelines as the South continued its massive resistance to integration. On June 11, 1963, Georgia Governor George C. Wallace stood in a doorway at the University of Alabama to block two African American students from registering. Wallace was flanked by Alabama state troopers. He had run for election the year before on a segregationist platform, promising his white followers that Alabama would maintain segregation.

Unlike President Eisenhower, who had delayed responding to the violence in Little Rock, Kennedy responded quickly. In a televised speech, he said the United States "will not be fully free until all of its citizens are free." He dispatched the National Guard to Alabama to end the standoff. Under pressure from the federal government, Wallace backed down. But in September, Wallace again tried to physically block African American students from entering Tuskegee High School in Huntsville, Alabama. Again President Kennedy deployed National Guard troops. Again Wallace backed down. Many white southerners seethed with anger at Kennedy for what they called federal government overreach.

✴   ✴   ✴   ✴   ✴   ✴   ✴   ✴   ✴   ✴   ✴   ✴   ✴   ✴   ✴

One day in late 1963, Marshall was at work in his office on the Second Circuit when he learned that John F. Kennedy had been shot and killed in Dallas, Texas. That same day, Vice President Lyndon B. Johnson, popularly known as LBJ, was sworn in as president.

Thurgood Marshall and LBJ had never met, but they knew of each other and admired each other. In 1944, in one of Marshall's Supreme Court victories, Marshall had made it possible for African Americans to vote in Texas primaries. Four years later, LBJ, a liberal Texan, ran for the U.S. Senate. He won with the support of African American voters, which wouldn't have happened without Marshall's voting rights work.

President Kennedy and his wife, Jacqueline, in the back seat of an open car, in Dallas shortly before the president was assassinated.

President Lyndon B. Johnson, 1964

Upon assuming office as the President of the United States, LBJ immediately pushed forward with a liberal agenda. In 1964 he signed into law the Civil Rights Act outlawing discrimination based on race, color, religion, gender, or national origin. The following year, in 1965, he signed into law the Voting Rights Act, primarily aimed at stopping practices, particularly in the South, that prevented African Americans and other minorities from voting.

* * * * * * * * * * * * * * *

ne day in July 1965, Marshall was in the judges' dining room at the courthouse. His bailiff came up and tapped him on the shoulder. Marshall was mildly annoyed. The judges weren't supposed to be bothered when they were in the dining room. Then he noticed his bailiff was red in the face.

"Fred, what in the world is wrong?" Marshall asked.

"The president wants to speak to you. He's on the phone!"

Marshall said, "The president of what?"

"The president of the United States!"

Marshall went downstairs, and sure enough, LBJ was on the line. "I want you to be my solicitor general," the president said.

> The job of the solicitor general of the United States is to represent the United States Department of Justice in the Supreme Court. The solicitor general manages a legal staff and large, complex caseload including the most pressing issues of the day. The soliciter general is thus one of the most prominent and powerful lawyers in the country.

"Well, Mr. President," Marshall said. "I'll have to think this over."

"Take all the time you want," LBJ said.

Marshall went home and talked to Cissy. The decision wasn't easy. A federal judgeship was a lifetime appointment. The job of solicitor general would last only until a new president was elected. On the other hand, the work of a solicitor general was more appealing to Marshall. He'd once again be arguing in the nation's highest court, handling the nation's most pressing cases.

Marshall still hadn't decided the next day when the phone rang. It was LBJ. He wanted to know what Marshall had decided.

"Well, Mr. President," Marshall said, "you said I had all the time I needed."

"You had it," he said.

Marshall accepted the job.

★ ★ ★ ★ ★ ★ ★ ★ ★ ★ ★ ★ ★ ★

The Marshall family moved to Washington, D.C., into a small townhouse in the Southwest Waterfront part of the city, and Marshall settled into his new job. When representing the government in the Supreme Court, Marshall's style was

Thurgood Marshall being sworn in as solicitor general with his family in attendance. Thurgood Jr., John, and Cissy stand next to President Johnson.

relaxed. While always deferential, he was conversational with the Supreme Court justices. He performed well, winning fourteen of the nineteen cases he handled as solicitor general.

He was often seen entering and leaving the White House for meetings with the president. The two men felt comfortable around each other. "You're very much like me," LBJ told Marshall once. As LBJ saw it, neither of them came from privilege. Both were rough-hewn and earthy. Both had a strong sense of social justice.

Cissy and Marshall enjoyed entertaining guests in their new home. Cissy kept their social calendar. Disciplining the boys also fell to Cissy because Thurgood refused to punish them. "I am not ever going to punish them for something that I did in my lifetime," Marshall said once. Cissy added, "So he never punished them, because he had done everything."

★ ★ ★ ★ ★ ★ ★ ★ ★ ★ ★ ★ ★ ★ ★

Meanwhile, the Warren Court was reshaping the law governing criminal procedures. The Court responded to appeals in which criminal defendants complained about their treatment at the hands of police. In 1966, the Supreme Court agreed to hear the appeal in a case called *Miranda v. Arizona*. The defendant, Ernesto Miranda, argued that his confession was illegal because the police, before questioning him, hadn't told him of his constitutional rights to remain silent and have a lawyer present. Miranda's case was grouped with three similar cases.

Thurgood Marshall was the government lawyer, so he had to defend the government—and the law enforcement officers. As a civil rights lawyer, he'd been able to select his cases and clients. Now he had no such luxury. He had to argue against his own views. He had seen firsthand how police often beat confessions out of African American men. He understood that preventing police from questioning a suspect without a lawyer present protected a defendant from having confessions beaten out of them and hence violating the Fifth Amendment of the Constitution by compelling him "to be a witness against himself." While he had no hand in the *Miranda* case itself, he did argue one of the cases with which Miranda's was grouped. He argued that an inflexible rule requiring officers to read suspects their rights would mean that often confessions that had not actually been coerced could be held invalid.

The Supreme Court ruled against the government, holding that police officers must read what have come to be called Miranda warnings: When the police make an arrest, they must inform the person of his or her rights, including the right to remain silent and the right to have a lawyer present before any further questioning occurs.

The Court's pronouncement that failure to administer the

warnings was a violation of a suspect's Fifth Amendment rights frustrated the nation's conservatives, because the Fifth Amendment said nothing at all about the police telling people their rights. The Fifth Amendment states that no person:

> *shall be compelled in any criminal case to be a witness against himself, nor be deprived of life, liberty, or property, without due process of law; nor shall private property be taken for public use, without just compensation.*

Conservatives thus denounced the decision as hampering police officers and making it too easy for lawbreakers to go unpunished for their crimes. They also insisted that the Warren Court was reading rights into the Constitution that were not there.

At about this time, the Republican Party adopted what it called the southern strategy, designed to lure white southerners from the Democratic to the Republican party. Given how razor-close elections were, they understood that drawing white southerners from the Democratic Party to the Republican Party would give the Republicans a clear majority. At the same time, the Republican leaders wanted to avoid overt racism. So they began calling for politicians to be "tough on crime." The slogan was neutral enough not to alarm conservatives who would not want to embrace anything racist but subtle enough to appeal to white southerners who visualized criminals as African American men and understood "tough on crime" to be a repudiation of the Warren Court's criminal procedure rulings.

In California, Republican Ronald Reagan adopted "tough on crime" as his campaign slogan when he ran for governor in 1966. Nixon, who would run for reelection again in 1968, would also adopt "tough on crime" as one of his campaign slogans.

Republican candidates also denounced what they called activist judges, which was another criticism of the Warren Court. By "activist," they meant that judges were creating laws by reading things into the Constitution. They also began slamming the federal government as too large and inefficient. Indeed, President Franklin D. Roosevelt's New Deal had dramatically increased the size of the federal government, which enraged a segment of the population that embraced a concept known as laissez-faire economics, which holds that the federal government should leave businesses and industries entirely alone and not regulate them.

The proponents of laissez-faire economics found themselves allied with white southerners who resented the expansion of the federal government and federal intrusion into local customs like segregation.

★　★　★　★　★　★　★　★　★　★　★　★　★　★　★

By the mid 1960s, the cultural revolution was in full swing. Rock and roll was the new music. Young African Americans began saying things like "Black is Beautiful." The word

The debate over whether the United States should have a strong central government or a weak one dates back to the founding of the nation. As secretary of the treasury, Alexander Hamilton looked for ways to create programs that would better the lives of the citizens. In the *Federalist Papers*, Hamilton commented that because people are creatures of habit, the more they become accustomed to having the government as part of their everyday lives, the more affection they will have for the government, in turn giving the government credibility and stabilizing the nation.

Thomas Jefferson, in contrast, believed that

"Negro" went out of style. First people said, "black," and later, "African American." Marshall was set in his ways. "'Black' is an adjective in my book," he said, "and the way I use it, sometimes I'll say 'African American people.' But if I'm talking about a person, I'm going to say 'a Negro,' because I was taught to say that, and I don't see any reason to change it."

Since the early 1960s, the United States had been sending soldiers to Vietnam to help the South Vietnamese fight against communist North Vietnam. As the war escalated, college

Hamilton's desire for a centralized government meant a loss of individual liberty. In his view, the entire reason the Revolutionary War had been fought was to free local governments from the tyranny of a distant, foreign, centralized government—and Jefferson considered anything outside of his home state of Virginia to be foreign. Jefferson imagined the United States as a loose association of strong states. Hamilton, by contrast, believed a strong economy required the states working together in cohesion, which meant a strong central government.

campuses erupted in anti-war protests. Young people said things like "Question authority." They denounced what they called police brutality. All of this horrified the nation's conservatives, who believed that all order was breaking down.

★ ★ ★ ★ ★ ★ ★ ★ ★ ★ ★ ★ ★ ★ ★

In June 1967, Supreme Court Justice Tom C. Clark announced that he would retire. It fell to President Johnson to name his successor.

The telephone in the Marshall home rang constantly. People had heard rumors. They'd heard that LBJ wanted to name an African American man to the United States Supreme Court. They'd heard that Marshall's name was on the short list. Cissy and Marshall didn't know if Marshall was being considered for the Supreme Court, so they told callers the truth: They had no idea.

On the morning of June 13, U.S. Attorney General Ramsey Clark visited Marshall's office. That day, as it turned out, Marshall had a meeting at the White House with some students. Clark suggested he arrive early and go to the main entrance. "The boss wants to see you," Clark explained.

"About what?" Marshall asked.

President Johnson nominates Thurgood Marshall to be an associate Supreme Court Justice.

"I actually don't know," said Clark.

Marshall did as he was told. When he arrived at his meeting with the president, LBJ said, "You know something, Thurgood, I'm going to put you on the Supreme Court."

Marshall had difficulty answering. "Well, thank you, sir."

Marshall and the president went into the Rose Garden, where Johnson made an announcement to the press. After Marshall and LBJ went back inside, Marshall asked if he could call his wife. "I think it would be better than for her to hear it on the radio."

Once Marshall had Cissy on the line, Marshall told her to sit down. He handed the phone to the president, who told Cissy, "I've just put your husband on the Supreme Court."

"I'm sure glad I'm sitting down," Cissy said. "Mr. President, I am simply speechless. Thank you for having so much faith in my husband."

II

A More Perfect Union

"We the People of the United States, in order to form a more perfect Union, establish Justice, insure domestic Tranquility, provide for the common defense, promote the general Welfare, and secure the Blessings of Liberty to ourselves and our Posterity, do ordain and establish this Constitution for the United States of America."

— Preamble to the U.S. Constitution

"The framers of our Constitution labored 'in order to form a more perfect union . . .' These were beautiful words, but at the same time, a Negro slave was but three-fifths of a man in the same Constitution."

— Thurgood Marshall

Senator Strom Thurmond from South Carolina settled on a strategy for attacking Thurgood Marshall and keeping him off the Supreme Court. He and his colleagues wouldn't go after Marshall's work on behalf of civil rights. That could too easily backfire by allowing the liberals and the press to smear them as racists. Instead, they would focus on Marshall's criminal cases and paint Marshall as a not-very-smart lawyer who was soft on crime. After all, Marshall had spent much of his career defending African American men accused of heinous crimes in the South.

On Thursday, July 13, 1967, Marshall arrived with Cissy at Room 2228 of the new Senate office building. Cameras were flashing. Spectators crowded into the room. Marshall took his seat.

The procedure was for the fifteen members of the Senate Judiciary Committee to question the nominee and determine whether he was fit to sit on the Supreme Court. If the committee voted yes, the matter would go to the full Senate for a vote.

The session opened with formalities and introductions. It was customary for the senators from the nominee's home state—in this case, New York—to introduce the nominee to the committee. "He's one of the most distinguished lawyers in the land," New York Senator Jacob Javits told the committee. "He has fought very hard to vindicate every aspect of the Constitution, with remarkable success . . ." Next, New York Senator Ted Kennedy introduced Marshall as "a man whose work has symbolized and spearheaded the struggle of millions of Americans before the law."

While Marshall had four avowed enemies on the committee—South Carolina Senator Strom Thurmond, Arkansas Senator John McClellan, North Carolina Senator Sam Ervin, and Mississippi Senator James Eastland—he also had a few staunch supporters. One of them was Senator Ted Kennedy, a brother of John F. Kennedy.

When the introductions were over, McClellan, the chair of the Senate Judiciary Committee, banged his gavel. He was eager to get started. He opened with a speech about rising crime rates. Then he asked Marshall, "Is my understanding correct that as of now, you do not think that the crime rate in this country has reached proportions where it endangers and jeopardizes our internal security?"

"I would say," Marshall responded, "that I have great faith in the ability of our country to meet any emergency, and I—"

"I am not asking what the country can meet," said McClellan. "I am trying to determine your attitude or sense, realization of the danger confronting this country with respect to this enemy of our security."

Marshall understood the implication. The "enemies of our security" were militant black groups, women's liberation protestors, and anti-war protestors, all of whom were leading the charge of a cultural revolution.

"I say in answer, Senator," Marshall said, "That I am as alarmed, I'm sure, as you are. But I am equally alarmed that whatever is to be done by governmental agencies to meet this situation has to be done within the framework of the U.S. Constitution. That is my only position."

McClellan asked him a question about a recent "5–4 Supreme Court decision." Marshall knew he was asking about *Miranda v. Arizona*, in which the judges had voted 5–4, with five liberal votes saying that the Constitution mandated that the police warn people about their rights when making arrests and four conservatives voting that it did not. Marshall also knew McClellan was trying to alert the conservative senators to the danger of putting yet another liberal vote onto the Supreme Court.

Marshall launched into an explanation of how the justices of the Supreme Court reach a decision. "The nine men meet in a conference room," he said, "and there is considerable give and take in the conference room. And where the vote ends up off by one, nobody knows how it started off."

There was a "gentle stirring in seats" as Marshall evaded the question. McClellan pushed him for a more direct answer on the power of one justice to sway a decision. Marshall dodged the question again by pointing out that he could not answer without commenting on the Supreme Court's recent ruling in *Miranda v. Arizona*, and that would not be appropriate.

"Do you subscribe to the philosophy," McClellan asked, "that the Fifth Amendment right to assistance of counsel requires that the counsel be present at a police lineup?"

McClellan evidently thought it absurd that the Fifth Amendment might mean the right to a lawyer in the early stages of an arrest.

"My answer would have to be the same," Marshall said. "That is part of the *Miranda* case."

"I do not care who it is that comes before this committee hereafter for the Supreme Court," McClellan said, "I am going to try to find out something about their philosophy . . . this is a fundamental principle."

Senator Eastland from Mississippi listened, jubilant. He thought Marshall's unwillingness to answer made clear that he was soft on crime. He also thought McClellan was effectively showing that Marshall "will not bring to the Court penetrating analysis or distinction of mind."

Senator Ted Kennedy asked permission to speak. He reminded the committee that, in addition to doing criminal defense work, the NAACP also did the important work of making sure African Americans had access to employment opportunities.

When it was Strom Thurmond's turn to ask questions, he asked Marshall for details about the ratification of the Fourteenth Amendment.

"Well, Senator," Marshall said, "I'm not a memory expert. I do research. And if you give me the question and let me get to my library, tomorrow morning, I'll give you the answer."

"I want the answer now," said Thurmond.

"I don't know," Marshall said.

"Who were the members of the committee that drafted the Fourteenth Amendment?" Strom Thurmond asked.

"I haven't the slightest idea," Marshall said. "I can find it out in the Congressional Library."

"You don't know?" Thurmond asked.

"No," Marshall said.

"You don't know?" Thurmond asked again.

"Nope, I don't know a one of them."

Thurmond looked at the assembled senators triumphantly.

Senator Ted Kennedy raised his hand and asked if Thurmond would yield for a question. Thurmond said he'd yield. "You know,

Senator," Kennedy said, "I, too, am interested—who *were* the members of the committee?"

Strom Thurmond didn't know the answer.

✶ ✶ ✶ ✶ ✶ ✶ ✶ ✶ ✶ ✶ ✶ ✶ ✶ ✶ ✶

While Marshall was focused on the questions and dodging verbal bullets, President Johnson was furiously lobbying other senators on the committee to vote in support of Marshall. It was often said in political circles that what LBJ wanted, LBJ got. A number of Democrats wanted to support the president, but they were afraid to go on record supporting an African American for the Supreme Court. LBJ persuaded them to abstain from voting.

At the conclusion of the questioning, the Senate Judiciary Committee voted. Eleven senators voted to approve Marshall's nomination, four voted against. When the matter then went to the full Senate, sixty-nine senators voted yes. Eleven voted no. Twenty senators did not vote.

✶ ✶ ✶ ✶ ✶ ✶ ✶ ✶ ✶ ✶ ✶ ✶ ✶ ✶ ✶

On Monday, October 2, 1967, in a public ceremony held at the courthouse on Foley Square, Thurgood Marshall—the

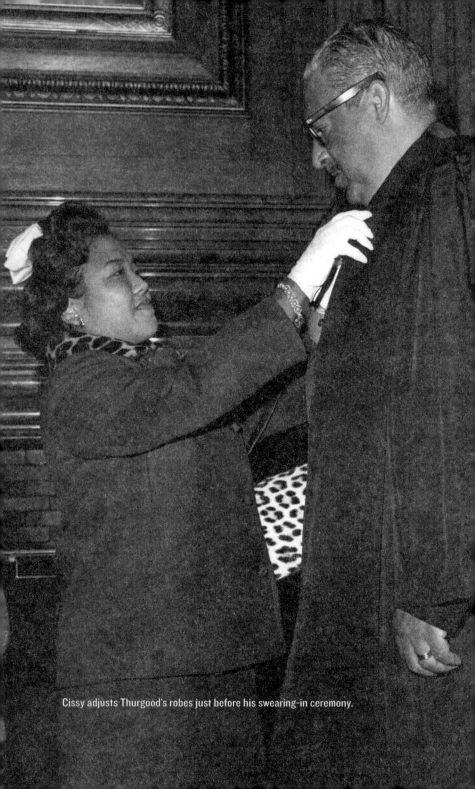

Cissy adjusts Thurgood's robes just before his swearing-in ceremony.

grandson of an enslaved man—was sworn in as the first African American Supreme Court justice. Just before the swearing in, Cissy proudly helped him adjust his black robe. Chief Justice Earl Warren administered the oath of office. Two hundred people attended the ceremony, including President Johnson, Senator Javits, William Hastie, Aubrey and Norma, and Marshall's sons.

✴   ✴   ✴   ✴   ✴   ✴   ✴   ✴   ✴   ✴   ✴   ✴   ✴   ✴   ✴

Because the United States Supreme Court interprets the Constitution, it is unlike any other court. It resolves fundamental questions about the scope and limits of personal liberty, relations between the races, and the limits of coequal branches of government. The Supreme Court is also responsible for keeping the nation's laws uniform. If all the lower courts agree on how to interpret a particular law, the Supreme Court is unlikely to grant review.

The Supreme Court operates as nine distinct and separate law offices with each justice hiring his or her own staff, including law clerks and messengers. The daily work of a Supreme Court justice largely consists of reading the briefs submitted by the lawyers, preparing to hear oral arguments, drafting decisions, and selecting the seventy-five or so cases the court will hear in a given term.

Marshall had appeared often enough before the Court that when he arrived as a justice, the others greeted him like a friend. Once each week, he joined a few of the others for lunch. His closest friend on the Court was Justice William Brennan, a liberal like Marshall. Marshall praised Brennan for having "unwavering commitment to . . . basic principles of civil rights and civil liberties."

One month after Marshall arrived on the Court, he wrote his first opinion. In a case called *Mempa v. Rhay*, he led the Court in a unanimous decision holding that a defendant in a criminal trial had the right to a lawyer at every stage of the proceedings—which included police lineups.

★　★　★　★　★　★　★　★　★　★　★　★　★　★　★

On April 4, 1968, Marshall was at work when he learned that Martin Luther King Jr. had been assassinated. The murder ignited an explosion of riots. Marshall called the White House to see if there was anything he could do. He had often given LBJ advice about his relationship to the African American community. When there seemed to be nothing he could do to help, he walked over to the Department of Justice to see Attorney General

Ramsey Clark. "Thurgood was profoundly affected," Clark said later. "Thurgood came in and . . . sat in the front office. I said, 'What are you doing?' He said, "I just wanted to be here in case there is anything I could do." Later, all Marshall could remember about the assassination was that "it was a rough night."

✷ ✷ ✷ ✷ ✷ ✷ ✷ ✷ ✷ ✷ ✷ ✷ ✷ ✷ ✷

Cissy decided she wanted more open space for Thurgood Jr. and John, so she found a house in Fairfax, Virginia, a Washington, D.C., suburb. Cissy loved the new neighborhood because it was walking distance from a lake and a bus line. A complication arose because the neighborhood she selected was all white, and banks refused to finance their mortgage—even though Marshall was a United States Supreme Court justice. She needed help from the attorney general to secure the loan.

About the time the family moved in late 1969, Earl Warren announced his retirement. Newly elected President Richard Nixon appointed Warren E. Burger as the new Chief Justice.

As Marshall relaxed into the job, his exuberance and sense of fun emerged. The Supreme Court was in many ways formal, even stuffy. Marshall, on the other hand, was known to greet Chief Justice Burger by asking, "What's shakin,' Chiefy Baby?"

One day a group of tourists took a wrong turn in the Supreme Court and ended up in the private elevator used by the justices. They assumed that the African American man inside was the elevator operator. One of the tourists asked to be taken to the first floor.

Marshall played along, answering in a humble southern accent. Later he insisted he had actually said, "Yes, Massah." He pushed the button, and the elevator headed to the first floor. When the elevator arrived on the first floor, Marshall held the door open for the tourists. Afterward, he got a hoot from telling the story.

In 1970, Marshall, who was then sixty-two, fell sick with a bad case of pneumonia. He ended up in the hospital. One day the doctor walked into his room and told him President Nixon wanted Marshall's medical records. Nixon wanted to know how close Marshall was to death so he would know how close he was to being able to appoint a conservative successor. Marshall told the doctor he could send a file with only two words written on the outside. The doctor agreed. Marshall wrote on the folder in large letters: NOT YET!

After Marshall recovered from pneumonia, he had a minor car accident while driving with his son Thurgood Jr. His son was unharmed. Marshall suffered a fractured ankle, which sparked speculation that he wouldn't be on the Court much longer. When people asked when he planned to retire, he said, "I have a lifetime appointment, and I intend to serve it. I expect to die at the age of one hundred and ten, shot by a jealous husband."

✶ ✶ ✶ ✶ ✶ ✶ ✶ ✶ ✶ ✶ ✶ ✶ ✶ ✶ ✶

In 1971, a case came to the Supreme Court called *Reed v. Reed*, a gender discrimination case. The Idaho Probate Code specified that "males must be preferred to females" in appointing the administrators of estates. After a teenage boy committed suicide, both parents wanted to be named administrator. The lower court appointed the boy's father, even though the mother was more qualified and even though the father had physically abused the boy and was accused of being partly responsible for his death.

Representing Sally Reed before the Supreme Court was Allen Derr—a lawyer clearly not up to the task. Derr stumbled his way through oral arguments, and, in what was clearly a case of nervousness, failed to answer basic questions put to him by the justices.

The legal brief submitted on behalf of Sally Reed, however,

Ruth Bader Ginsburg as a law professor and lawyer, 1977

was brilliant. The brief was written by an unknown female law professor from Rutgers Law School. Her name was Ruth Bader Ginsburg. She argued that the Fourteenth Amendment included women and that laws that discriminated on the basis of sex violated the equal protection clause.

In the late 1960s, when Ruth Bader Ginsburg took on the task of changing the laws regarding women, she faced the same obstacles the NAACP had faced in the 1930s. The Supreme Court in the nineteenth century had ruled that women were not persons under the Fourteenth Amendment by comparing them to young children and mentally incompetent adults.

Ginsburg, later called the Thurgood Marshall of the women's rights movement, modeled her strategy for gaining equality for women on the NAACP's strategy for ending segregation. She started on the fringes, with easy cases that

Marshall recognized that discrimination on the basis of sex "posed for the Courts the specter of forms of discrimination which it implicitly recognized to have deep social and legal roots without necessarily having any basis in actual differences." He joined the other justices in ruling unanimously for Sally Reed. The ruling was a narrow one, forbidding only a mandatory preference for men—but for the first time since the ratification of the Fourteenth Amendment, the Court reversed a statute as violating the equal protection clause as applied to women.

didn't upset the status quo—like *Reed v. Reed*—while educating courts and the public about the harm of gender discrimination.

The victory in *Reed v. Reed* was just the beginning of Ginsburg's legal campaign for women's rights. On the books were literally hundreds of statutes barring women from almost all aspects of public life. Many of the laws were rooted in deeply held stereotypes about women, which would not be easy to overcome. Like Thurgood Marshall had done for African American rights, Ginsburg tirelessly brought cases that chipped away at women's inferior legal status with her eye on the grand prize: equal rights for women in all areas of American life.

★   ★   ★   ★   ★   ★   ★   ★   ★   ★   ★   ★   ★   ★

On August 8, 1972, Aubrey—who had never fully recovered his health after coming down with tuberculosis—died in Wilmington, Delaware, at the age of sixty-seven. Marshall and Aubrey had never been close, and in recent years, they had drifted even further apart. According to family rumor, Aubrey had been a little jealous of Marshall's success. Marshall and Cissy attended Aubrey's funeral in Wilmington, Delaware.

About that time, one of the Supreme Court's liberal justices, John Harlan, died. President Nixon appointed his replacement: William Rehnquist, who, as a young law clerk working on the Supreme Court in 1952, had written a memo arguing that *Plessy v. Ferguson* was right and should be reaffirmed. In 1975, Nixon's successor, Republican President Gerald Ford, appointed another conservative, John Paul Stevens.

The conservatives, Marshall's ideological opponents, were once again a majority on the Court. Marshall and the remaining liberal justices were powerless as their conservative colleagues began rolling back progress from the 1950s and 1960s.

In 1979, the Supreme Court heard a challenge to the conditions under which defendants were held in jail prior to their trials. The detainees were subject to harsh confinement, including crowded conditions and rules limiting what reading material they were permitted. They were also subjected to humiliating body searches. The prisoners claimed that the presumption of innocence and due process was violated, as they were subject to what amounted to harsh punishment but had not yet been found guilty of crimes. They wanted pretrial incarceration to be less harsh.

To Marshall's horror, a five-justice majority ruled that harsh pretrial detentions did not violate the Constitution. In a case called *Bell v. Wolfish,* the majority of justices ruled that unless the jailors *intended* to punish the inmates, there were no constitutional violations if the rules were harsh. The problem was that proving that the intention was to punish was almost impossible. Marshall wrote what is known as a dissenting opinion—justices who disagree with the majority opinion can write their own dissents explaining why they disagree. Marshall slammed the decision as allowing "arbitrary or purposeless" harshness as long as there was no "intent" to punish.

In *City of Mobile v. Bolden*, the Court heard a challenge to a Mobile, Alabama, voting procedure that unfairly stripped

Thurgood Marshall's official Supreme Court portrait, 1976

power from African American citizens by electing officials "at large"—meaning that all the voters decided on all the officials—instead of permitting each district to elect its own officials. Had each district been able to elect its own, the city's largely African American district would be able to elect its own official, and one of the city commissioners would likely have been African American. Instead, because the officials were elected at large, all the officials were white. The Supreme Court held that the Fifteenth Amendment guaranteeing African Americans the right to vote did not give the Court power to overturn local election procedures unless it could be proven that the lawmakers had been motivated by a desire to discriminate. This, too, was almost impossible to prove.

Then, in 1985, the Supreme Court heard an appeal from a murder case in Florida. At the sentencing, the appointed attorney failed to do the basics: He failed to seek out character witnesses or request a psychiatric evaluation for his client. The trial court sentenced the defendant to death because it found no mitigating circumstances. The issue on appeal before the Supreme Court was whether the death penalty should be reversed on the grounds that the defendant's Sixth Amendment right to a lawyer had been violated because his lawyer had been incompetent.

Thurgood was distressed when the conservative majority held that there wasn't enough evidence that the death penalty resulted from inadequate counsel, so they upheld the death penalty. Both he and Brennan wrote stinging dissents.

Marshall grew increasingly cross and irritable as he listened to his conservative colleagues insist that the Constitution must be enforced as intended in the eighteenth century by the founding fathers. Given the fact that the founders understood that the Constitution would maintain the institution of slavery, Marshall found these arguments offensive. He was curt with lawyers who made arguments he found objectionable. "Once in a while he'll explode," Cissy said, when asked about her husband's frustration with the conservative court. "I wish he would explode more and get it out of his system. But he keeps a lot in."

Like the Supreme Court, the Republican Party had undergone a metamorphosis. The southern strategy had succeeded in drawing a majority of white southerners into the Republican Party. When the Ku Klux Klan found a home on the far-right-wing fringes of the Republican Party, the realignment of the parties was complete. The party of Lincoln was now the party of the Ku Klux Klan. The Democratic Party—which had once been the party of the Confederacy—had become the party of urban America, minorities, and liberal communities.

By this time, the Marshall boys were grown. Thurgood Marshall Jr. earned his college degree from the University of Virginia. After graduating college, he enrolled in the University of Virginia School of Law. He began his legal career three years later with the prestigious position of law clerk to Judge Barrington D. Parker, a judge on the D.C. federal district court. Marshall and Cissy's younger son, John, earned his undergraduate degree from Georgetown University, and afterward, a certificate in administration of justice from Virginia Commonwealth University. He served in the Virginia state police. Later he would become Virginia secretary of public safety.

With the boys grown and out of the house, Cissy occupied herself with volunteer work. She was on the board of directors of the Legal Defense Fund and Traveler's Aid, a liberal organization that provided services to people who were stranded, vulnerable, and needed help getting home.

Marshall was growing tired. By this time, he walked with a cane and rarely went out in the evenings. He suffered from glaucoma. When he wasn't at the Court, he was at home. His voice deepened so that at times it sounded like a low growl.

★ ★ ★ ★ ★ ★ ★ ★ ★ ★ ★ ★ ★ ★

America celebrated the two hundredth anniversary of the ratification of the Constitution in May 1987. Thurgood Marshall was seventy-nine years old. The bicentennial celebration was a time of flag-waving and praising the genius of the founding fathers in establishing the guiding legal principles in the United States.

Thurgood Marshall was invited to give a bicentennial speech in Hawaii. Cissy and Marshall flew to Hawaii for the event. Marshall proceeded to give what was, for many, a shocking speech. He declared that the original Constitution as ratified two hundred years earlier was "defective from the start" because it allowed slavery and denied women the right to vote. It had taken a "bloody Civil War" to abolish slavery. The nation, he declared,

Cissy and Marshall, undated

208

was still struggling with the consequences of an initial Constitution that treated some of its citizens as less than human.

His critical remarks about the Constitution were flashed across the country in news broadcasts. His conservative colleagues understood that he had taken a swipe at their theory of originalism. His critics painted him as unpatriotic. He felt less comfortable on the Court, feeling that he had little in common with his more conservative colleagues.

★ ★ ★ ★ ★ ★ ★ ★ ★ ★ ★ ★ ★ ★

In 1990, Marshall agreed to give a speech at the Sheraton Washington Hotel. He walked slowly, evidently in pain. As he trudged to the ballroom, African American employees of the hotel—bellhops and waiters—heard he was coming, so they streamed out to catch a glimpse of him. Some of the older African American employees, gazing at Marshall, had tears in their eyes.

One white employee, startled by the emotion of his coworkers, tapped an African American coworker on the arm. "What's going on? Who is that guy?"

"That's Thurgood Marshall."

The white employee answered uncertainly: "He's one of those Supreme Court judges, right?"

✦ ✦ ✦ ✦ ✦ ✦ ✦ ✦ ✦ ✦ ✦ ✦ ✦ ✦ ✦

By June 1991, Marshall knew he couldn't go on working. He told his colleagues that he planned to retire. Chief Justice Rehnquist, who had long been one of Marshall's ideological opponents, in an uncharacteristic display of affection, went to him and gave him a hug.

The next day, on June 27, 1991, Marshall sent a letter to President George H. W. Bush, which was immediately released to the press:

My Dear Mr. President:

The strenuous demands of Court work and its related duties required or expected of a Justice appear at this time to be incompatible with my advancing age and medical condition. I, therefore, retire as an Associate Justice of the Supreme Court of the United States when my successor is qualified.

Respectfully, Thurgood Marshall

At a press conference, Marshall fielded questions from reporters. One reporter asked him what was wrong with him. "What's wrong with me?" Marshall said. "I'm old. I'm getting old and coming apart." Another asked him how he made the decision to retire. He said, "I looked at the facts and the law. I put them together and came up with an opinion."

A reporter asked him what he thought was the greatest challenge now facing the Supreme Court. He said, "To get along without me."

Another question was: How do you want to be remembered? Marshall said, "He did what he could with what he had."

★　★　★　★　★　★　★　★　★　★　★　★　★　★

On January 21, 1992, Marshall was taken to Bethesda Naval Medical Center in Maryland. Three days later, in the early-morning hours, he died of heart failure. He was eighty-four years old.

His body was placed in a pine casket on a bier that had once held Abraham Lincoln's body. The casket, draped with an American flag, lay in state in the Court's Great Hall. The January winds were bitterly cold, but a long line of mourners stretched down the steps of the Supreme Court and around the block. So many people came that the chief justice ordered the building kept open until late into the night so all the mourners could be accommodated. Eighteen thousand people paid their respects that day. Many stopped to weep. Some left roses.

Others left copies of Marshall's brief from *Brown v. Board of Education.*

One of the speakers was Washington, D.C., lawyer Vernon Jordan, who said, "We thank you, Thurgood . . . your voice is stilled, but your message lives. Indeed, you have altered America irrevocably and forever."

Legacy

> "We make movies about Malcolm X, we get a holiday
> to honor Dr. Martin Luther King, but every day we live
> with the legacy of Justice Thurgood Marshall."
>
> —*from an editorial by
> the* Washington Afro-American *after
> Thurgood Marshall's death*

Brown v. Board of Education is one of the most important legal cases in United States history. It opened
the door to racial equality and set in motion a chain
of events that forever altered race relations in America. Because it also helped usher in the women's
rights movement, *Brown v. Board of Education* sparked a period
of rapid changes. Prior to *Brown v. Board of Education*, African

Before the civil rights movement, members of Congress were almost entirely white and
male. This image was taken in January 1939.

By 2018, though still overwhelmingly white and male, the House of Representatives had grown more diverse. Here is the newly elected House of Representatives in that year.

Americans, members of other minority groups, or women occasionally achieved professional success—but they were the notable exceptions. After the modern civil rights and women's rights movements, minorities and women began entering professions and government positions in greater numbers.

In 2008, America elected its first African American president, Barack Obama. By 2019, more than one in five voting members of the U.S. House of Representatives and Senate were members of a racial or ethnic minority, making the 116th Congress (the result of the 2018 midterm elections) the most diverse in United States history.

Members of racial minorities also moved into professions such as medicine and law in greater numbers. As of 2018, the Association of American Colleges and Universities reported that less than 20 percent of the nation's college professors are people of color. While this still lagged behind the population as a whole (people of color comprise about a third of the population of the United States), African Americans were becoming university professors in state and private universities in numbers unimaginable when Charles Houston and Thurgood Marshall set out on their quest to desegregate schools.

Liberals cheered the changes made possible by Thurgood

Marshall's work and looked forward to a future of even greater inclusiveness. After Ruth Bader Ginsburg became a Supreme Court justice in 1993, she explained the liberal view in this way: In the preamble to the Constitution, the phrase "we the people" is linked to the phrase "a more perfect union"; therefore, as more people come to be included in "we the people," the union becomes more perfect.

Those on the far right have the opposite view. They look back with nostalgia to a time they think America was great—when white men held nearly every position of authority and when life seemed more structured and orderly. Many on the far right believe nature forms a hierarchy and that disrupting the hierarchy creates dangerous chaos. The civil rights and women's rights movement disrupted what they saw as a well-structured society. Many look back longingly to an America of yesteryear. The first American politician to use the phrase "make America great again" was Ronald Reagan in 1980. Donald Trump adopted "Make America Great Again" as the slogan of his presidential campaign in 2016. The slogan promises a return to a golden, bygone era.

In the view of the liberals, Thurgood Marshall moved the country forward, because he "rethreaded the Constitution itself, stitching the Negro, at long last, into the fabric of the nation."

The theory of contemporary ratification—interpreting the Constitution in light of what its concepts should mean today instead of as they were intended in 1789—was the doctrine that shattered paternalism and allowed for increasing diversity in American public life. For conservatives and originalists, Marshall, in advocating the theory of contemporary ratification, was putting forward a repugnant view of the Constitution, which cast a slur on the founding fathers and removed power from the states and local communities, giving it instead to the federal government.

Will the federal government continue to be a strong and unifying force in America, as Alexander Hamilton envisioned, or will state governments once again assert more power?

Will America continue to move toward greater inclusiveness, as the liberals envision? Or will America loop backward and once more adopt the culture of a previous era?

The answers to those questions will be decided by you. You hold the future in your hands.

The Supreme Court in 2019. Front row, left to right: Associate Justice Stephen G. Breyer, Associate Justice Clarence Thomas, Chief Justice John G. Roberts Jr., Associate Justice Ruth Bader Ginsburg, Associate Justice Samuel A. Alito. Back row: Associate Justice Neil M. Gorsuch, Associate Justice Sonia Sotomayor, Associate Justice Elena Kagan, Associate Justice Brett M. Kavanaugh.

Timeline

1908 ✶ Thurgood Marshall, whose given name was Thoroughgood Marshall, is born in Baltimore, Maryland.

1925 ✶ Thurgood graduates high school and enrolls as a freshman at Lincoln University in Pennsylvania.

1929 ✶ SEPTEMBER 4: Thurgood marries Vivian (Buster) Burney.

1930 ✶ Marshall graduates with honors from Lincoln University.

1933 ✶ Marshall graduates cum laude from Howard Law School.

1935 ✶ Marshall wins his first major civil rights case, *Murray v. Pearson.*

1936 ✶ Marshall becomes legal counsel for the NAACP. In October, he moves to New York City.

1938 ✶ The Supreme Court orders the University of Missouri to admit an African American law student.

1940 ✶ Marshall takes Charles Houston's place as special counsel to the NAACP.

      ✶ Marshall wins a Supreme Court victory (first of twenty-nine), *Chambers v. Florida.*

1954 ✶ Marshall wins *Brown v. Board of Education.*

      ✶ Buster is diagnosed with cancer, the disease that will take her life.

1955 ✶ Marshall marries Cecilia (Cissy) Suyat.

1956 ✶ AUGUST 12: The Marshalls' son Thurgood Jr. is born.

1958 ✶ JULY 6: The Marshalls' son John is born.

Timeline

1961 ✶ President John F. Kennedy appoints Marshall as a federal circuit judge.

1965 ✶ President Lyndon B. Johnson appoints Marshall as U.S. Solicitor General.

1967 ✶ President Lyndon B. Johnson appoints Marshall as the first African American Supreme Court justice.

1991 ✶ Marshall retires from the Supreme Court.

1993 ✶ Marshall dies at the age of eighty-four.

Selected Writings of Thurgood Marshall

*Excerpt from
remarks Thurgood Marshall
made at the Second Circuit
Judicial Conference,
May 1980*

The Constitution embodies the very spirit of democratic government. When the Founding Fathers sat down to draft the instrument that would form the framework for this country, they did far more than establish a series of legal precepts, although of course those legal precepts are vital rights of all Americans. The Constitution also sets forth basic principles which are the very essence of the United States. The primary principle is equality. The Fifth Amendment provides that "no person" shall be deprived of life, liberty, or property without due process of law. This was reaffirmed in the Fourteenth Amendment, which bans the denial of equal protection of the laws "to any person." The very first truth which we declared self-evident in the Declaration of Independence was that "all men are created equal." Every person has the same "unalienable rights" of life, liberty, and the pursuit of happiness, and all persons are to be treated with the respect and decency which those inalienable rights demand.

A related principle is participation in the governing process. It was "we the people," not some smaller or more elite group, who established the Constitution "in order to form a more perfect union." As was stated in the Declaration of Independence, "Governments are instituted among men, deriving their just powers from the consent of the governed." Participation recognizes the moral worth of each individual, and in this way shows again that all persons are equal.

From the very beginning of this Nation, therefore, we have recognized that in order to achieve the good society, there must be equality, there must be participation in the governing process, and accordingly there must be a government of laws rather than of men. Such a society will be just, for every member will be treated with equal respect and dignity.

It is the responsibility of the judiciary to make sure that we remain a government of laws and that all persons are equal under those laws. This is the essence of justice. It is a weighty responsibility, but we are uniquely qualified for the task under our Constitutional scheme.

There are three major differences between the judiciary and the other branches of government. First, the executive and legislature of necessity must be preoccupied with the needs of the moment. The economy desperately needs attention, and international crises occur almost daily. Prompt action is required. Day-to-day decisions must be made through a process of accommodation among diverse political groups in order to reach acceptable results which may be put into operation quickly. Compromise is an essential element of the political process. Second, the political branches are designed to function through the clash of partisan interests. The members of the executive and legislature are supposed to be representative of the interests of their electorate, to make sure that in the compromises which are made their groups are fairly treated. Third, the other branches in large measure deal in abstractions. The legislature passes laws of general application based on composites and projections. The executive has the responsibility to enforce those laws on a broad scale.

In the courts, by contrast, the emphasis is on the individual, impartiality is required, and political compromise has no role at all. Judges are supposed to be reflective, considering the controversy before them in light of the broader legal schemes, Constitutional and otherwise, which guide the country. Decisions traditionally are justified by opinions announcing reasoning derived from earlier cases and established principles; raw political power is never a sufficient justification for any judicial decision. Constitutional rights should never be compromised by the courts in the name of expediency . . .

✶ ✶ ✶ ✶ ✶ ✶ ✶ ✶ ✶ ✶ ✶ ✶ ✶ ✶ ✶

Opening paragraph from the "Summary of the Argument" from Thurgood Marshall's Supreme Court Brief in Brown v. Board of Education (argument for the Kansas plaintiffs appellants)

The Fourteenth Amendment precludes a state from imposing distinctions or classifications based upon race and color alone. The State of Kansas has no power thereunder to use race as a factor in affording educational opportunities to its citizens. Racial segregation in public schools reduces the benefits of public education to one group solely on the basis of race and color and is a constitutionally proscribed distinction. Even assuming that the segregated schools attended by appellants are not inferior to other elementary schools in Topeka with respect to physical facilities, instruction, and courses of study, unconstitutional inequality inheres in the retardation of intellectual development and distortion of personality which Negro children suffer as a result of enforced isolation in school from the general public school population. Such injury and inequality are established as facts on this appeal by the uncontested findings of the District Court.

Notes

Note: Wherever an individual is quoted having used a profanity, a dash is used in place of the word, like this: d—

Prologue:
A Public Enemy

3   "was considered a public enemy of the South": Haygood, 19.
4   "I believe he has already . . . valuable service to the country": Williams, 335.
5   "Please, sir . . . so many feel as we do": Williams, 5618.

Chapter 1:
Way Up South

6   "It was taken for granted . . . of the home": Gibson, 541.
6   "baddest N— in the whole state of Maryland": Kluger, 173.
6   "But we all know that he really came from the toughest part of the Congo": Kluger, 173–174.
7   "Now, look . . . I'm proud of a guy like that": Marshall, *His Speeches*, 418–419.
8   "way up South": Marshall, *His Speeches*, 412.
10 "This went on for days . . . sit-down strike in Maryland": Kluger, 173–174.
10 "The door was left open . . . Nobody ever did": Marshall, *His Speeches*, 419.
13 "If somebody calls you . . . right then and there": Williams, 393.
13 "That's very black of you": Marshall, *His Speeches*, 415.
13 "got a bang out of shocking white people": Gibson, 484.

Notes

13 "My father was the noisiest . . . mother was by far the strongest": Marshall, *His Speeches*, 415.

14 "get that cat out of here": Williams, 609.

14 "Our home got to be known as the 'Friendly Inn'": Williams, 609.

14 "In the department stores . . . h— out": Marshall, *His Speeches*, 412.

15 "There were no toilet facilities . . . try to get home": Marshall, *His Speeches*, 412

16 "a jolly boy . . . going on inside of him": Kluger, 173.

17 "In Baltimore . . call me:": Crowe, 52.

17 "They were practically . . . I remember you": Marshall, *His Speeches*, 412.

18 "If anybody called me a 'N—' I fought 'em": Williams, 708.

18 "We had the most violent . . . at the dinner table": Marshall, 414.

18 "He did it by . . . turned me into one": Gibson, 507.

20 "He could outtalk and out-argue anybody": Gibson, 796.

21 "Black boy, why don't you just shut your mouth, you're going to talk yourself into the electric chair": Williams, 827.

22 "Don't push . . . talk to me like that": Williams, 393. The same story, worded differently, is given in Marshall, 412. Marshall tended to vary stories slightly with the retelling—just small details. I credited the interviews given earlier in his life and closer to the events.

22 "Forget about them . . . he sure did": Williams, 408.

23 "I never felt good around them . . . grin and bear it": Williams, 990.

24 "He didn't aim . . . that way": Williams, 816.

24 "Before I left that school, I knew the whole thing by heart": Williams, 816.

26 "Get your clothes. You're fired": Williams, 954

27 "What do you plan . . . A lawyer" Williams, 923.

Chapter 2:
College Days

28 "None of us . . . up our boots:" Marshall said this in response to Clarence Thomas, a conservative African American Supreme Court nominee who claimed to have pulled himself up by his bootstraps. NAACP, also quoted in the *Record of the Association of the Bar of the City of New York*, vol. 57, p. 470.

29 "I just eased along . . . enough to pass": Marshall, *His Speeches*, 414.

30 "Ah, the boys are home": Marshall, *His Speeches*, 414.

30 "Hey, N— I want service at this table": Williams, 1014.

31 "The minute . . . bust him in the nose": Williams, 1026.

31 "further intermixing . . . is desirable": Haygood, 43.

33 "How do you know it . . . something about it": Marshall, *His Speeches*, 416.

34 "he was so busy arguing and debating with everyone at the table": Williams, 1141.

34 "First we decided to get married . . . my last semester": Gibson, 1223.

36 "Howard Law . . . other school": Haygood, 46.

Chapter 3:
Top Man in the Class

37 "I never worked hard . . . ship out": Crowe, 91.

38 "Every man here . . . that's murder!": Marshall, *His Speeches*, 271.

38 "I'll never be satisfied . . . law books": Marshall, *His Speeches*, 272.

38 "I'd got the horsing around . . . way deep": Crowe, 88.

39 "This was what . . . seven days a week": Haygood, 49.

39 "Every time . . . No, never": Williams, 1270.

42 "hell-bent on establishing . . . in the whole country": Marshall, *His Speeches*, 420.

43 "Men, you've got to be . . . than he is": Social engineer or parasite: Gibson, 4138

43 "He rightfully . . . other nice names": Marshall, *His Speeches*, 272.

44 "I came out top man": Marshall, *His Speeches*, 414.

45 "In the library . . . that didn't hurt": Marshall, *His Speeches*, 414.

46 "as if they were partners in an elite black law firm": Williams, 1276.

46 "We started . . . We studied it": Marshall, *His Speeches*, 414.

49 "Laws permitting . . . race to the other": *Plessy v. Ferguson.*

50 "promotes the evenhanded . . . judicial process": *Kimble v. Marvel Enterprises* 576 U.S.___2015, available here: www.supremecourt.gov/opinions/14pdf/13-720_jiel.pdf.

51 "I couldn't wait to get out and practice": Marshall, *His Speeches*, 417.

Chapter 4:
The Equalization Strategy

55 "In recognizing the humanity . . . highest tribute": Williams, 7224.

55 "Young man . . . and we'll talk": Williams, 1351.

59 "I don't have a nickel . . . for nothing": Crowe, 100.

59 "I've got to stop that crap right now": Williams, 1377.

59 "wasn't a good way to make a living": Crowe, 100.

59 "Go ahead . . . back to me anyhow": Williams, 1536.

61 "The South would go broke paying for truly equal dual systems": Williams, 1628.

63 "Dear Charlie . . . as soon as possible": Kluger, 196.

65 "a separate institution of higher learning for the education of Negroes": Gibson, 2862.

70 "I wish to be quoted as saying . . . class in the law school": Crowe, 3197.

Notes

70 "epoch making": Haygood, 59.

70 "Don't Shout Too Soon": Kluger, 195.

70 "to the presence among them . . . class A college": Kluger, 193.

71 "adolescents going through the ordinary college mill and eager only to dance and [kiss]": Williams, 1665.

73 "exceedingly cordial and so were professors": Williams, 1699.

Chapter 5:
A Social Engineer

74 "A child born . . . worth fighting for": Widely quoted, including the Library of Congress website: www.loc.gov/teachers/ classroommaterials/presentationsandactivities/presentations/ immigration/alt/african_voc_answers.html; in Marshall's collective works, he paraphrases what he "always" says on page 204.

77 "break down the traits of the state of Maryland": Williams, 1723.

79 "looked a little strange . . . not say anything": Kluger, 203.

79 "It is beyond . . . ready for the appeal": Kluger, 204.

79 "I don't know of anybody . . . preparation of cases": Williams, 1817.

80 "I whooped and hollered . . . if I was dying": Crowe, 112.

80 "I will be indebted . . . dreamed of doing": Williams, 1817.

81 "gathered up our rages . . . near the Polo Grounds": Crowe, 111.

82 "Everyone loved Thurgood . . . energy and warmth": Kluger, 221.

82 "School situation is terrible . . . typical Uncle Tom": Williams, 2016.

83 "his poorest white teacher was better than the best colored teacher": Williams, 1918.

83 "had always been African Americans' work": Williams, 1931.

85 "monstrous reality . . . court of law": *West Texas Tribune*, Thurgood Marshall and the West Texas NAACP Connection.

Notes

85 "personally take him out and kick the sh— out of him": Williams, 2156.

85 "I sort of considered . . . you will not be injured": Williams, 2156.

85 "boy" . . . "right man for the job" . . . "I've got you now!": Williams, 2127.

86 "Fella . . . just stay right where you are": Williams, 2169.

87 "A state could not export its Fourteenth Amendment responsibilities": Ripple, 475.

Chapter 6: Speaking Out

89 "Where you see wrong . . . Go to it": Marshall, 279.

89 "I am much more of an outside man than an inside man": Williams, 2083.

90 "render legal aid gratuitously to such Negroes as may appear to be worthy": Haygood, 62.

91 "If it happens . . . it happens": Crowe, 132.

91 "I was out there . . . the next train": Owen Fiss, *Legacy of Thurgood Marshall*, 49.

95 "There's the bones . . . more torture": Crowe, 122.

97 "uppity New York . . . make trouble": Crowe, 124.

97 "I didn't want anyone . . . and rejoice": Crowe, 124.

98 "Oh, yes. . . whipping you!": Williams, 2439.

98 "I thought it would refresh his mind . . . his 'N— beater'": Williams, 2439.

100 "it clearly shows . . . position to appeal": Williams, 2452.

102 "constitutional requirement of due process of law a meaningless symbol": *Chambers v. Florida*, 309 U.S. 227 (1940).

102 "far and away . . . our highest Court": Rosen, 141.

103 "the procure . . . have completely worn off": Williams, 2482.

Chapter 7:
Mr. Civil Rights

104 "Racism separates . . . no one benefits from racism": Marshall, *Supreme Justice*, 312.

104 "Thurgood's coming . . . white men's courtrooms": Haygood, 62.

105 "we need to feel in our own minds . . . Anybody": Kluger, 222.

105 "I never hesitated to pick other people's brains—brains I didn't have": Kluger, 221.

105–109 One of his most harrowing experiences . . . reached Nashville safely: Many details from this story were taken from a videotaped interview with Dr. Carol Anderson of Emory University, available here: www.youtube.com/watch?v=qeCjvqFKxMo, www.c-span .org/video/?4519-1/tribute-justice-thurgood-marshall. There are numerous retellings of this story with slightly different details. The story varies slightly with each retelling simply because different details are included. I have used a combination of the C-SPAN video and Marshall's account as given in his Reminiscences, included in Marshall, 428.

110 "Look, just two sets of people . . . will be there, unharmed": Haygood, 68.

111 "Thurgood, you know d— good and well that's a lie": Williams, 1898.

112 "our greatest civil liberties . . . U.S. Supreme Court": Williams, 3925.

112 "make a big fuss about it": Williams, 3901.

116 "Thurgood's wonderful . . . look at him go": Haygood, 79.

117 "We'd like to help you fellas . . . Cumberland High School": Kluger, 476.

117 "The first little . . . blow his brains out": Kluger, 476.

Notes

118 "We ain't got no money to buy a bus for your n— children": Kluger, 4.

122 "Sweatt's got two chances: slim and none": Williams, 9523.

124 "All we ask in the South . . . work it out [ourselves]": Williams, 3765.

124 "Whatever credit is given him is not enough": Williams, 3779.

125 "We won the big one": Williams, 3793.

Chapter 8: Brown v. Board of Education

127 "We are convinced . . . Jim Crow citadel": Williams, 3737.

129 "You know that this is . . . first of this week": Kluger, 467.

132 "They came in their jalopy cars . . . miles to be here": Williams, 4093.

135 "Thurgood had . . . and make it his": Williams, 4220.

136 "He's aged so much . . . he's set himself": Haygood, 79.

137 "It's very important to have a civil relationship with your opponent": Williams 4394.

138 "No, sir . . . perpetuated in the statutes": Marshall, *His Speeches*, 25.

138 "Frankfurter was a smart aleck, you know": Williams, 4435.

138 "We shall get a finer . . . ridiculed and hated": Williams, 4449.

143 "to keep people who were formerly in slavery . . . as near that stage as is possible": Williams, 4597.

143 "came on like a locomotive": Williams, 4597.

143 "These same kids . . . play ball together": Kluger, 667.

144 "We conclude . . . inherently unequal" . . . "I was so happy I was numb": Crowe, 167.

145 "We hit the jackpot": Williams, 4638.

146 "picked up our son Bill . . . just won a biggie": Williams, 4654.

146 "I don't remember having . . . so many years:" Kluger, 681.

Chapter 9:
Massive Resistance

147 "What is striking . . . equality by law": Marshall, 283.

147 "The South . . . the Court": Williams, 4700.

147 "the rights of the states, as guaranteed by the Constitution, to direct their most vital local affairs": Williams, 4107.

147 "first step toward national suicide": Williams, 4694–4711.

148 "I personally think the decision was wrong": Williams, 4711.

148 "If I had my life . . . to help [Thurgood] make good": Williams, 4813.

148 "During this time . . . cadaverous in appearance": Haygood, 81.

149 "He took her death very, very hard": Williams, 4786.

150 "blessing . . . watching over me": LOC interview.

150 "How's the weather down there . . . on a chair": "Thurgood Marshall's interracial love."

152 "We were advising them . . . never heard of him until then": Marshall, 470.

152 "We were tired . . . feet of oppression": Williams, 5036.

154 "I used to have . . . jail for it": Marshall, *His Speeches*, 470.

158 "street theater": Williams, 5064.

158 "a teakettle about to explode": Williams, 5105.

158 "blood will run in the street": Williams, 5401.

160 "Lynch her! Lynch her!": Williams, 5401.

161 The videotapes played widely on television: Footage has been made available on YouTube by the Oklahoma Historical Society. www .youtube.com/watch?v=c_I8846NL-U.

162 "If you mean by Civil War . . . law of the land": Interview Thurgood Marshall (Mike Wallace), Tuesday, April 16, 1957, available on YouTube, www.youtube.com/watch?v=IoPLitU6jVg.

162 "should have sat down and planned . . . they could think of": Williams, 5415.

Notes

Chapter 10:
Judge Marshall

164 "It is the responsibility of the judiciary . . . essence of justice":
Marshall, *His Speeches*, 183.

165 "Thurgood stormed . . . crazy colored students": Marshall, 183.

168 "You know, they tell me everybody in the world got Martin Luther
King Jr. out but the lawyer": Williams, 5932.

172 "will not be fully free until all of its citizens are free": Kennedy's
June 11, 1963 speech addressing the nation after the racial turmoil in
Alabama is available here: www.nbcnews.com/id/52176687/t/watch-
jfks-civil-rights-speech-years-ago/#.XEDdVy2ZNpI.

175 "Fred, what in the world . . . I want you to be my solicitor general":
Interview, January 10, 1969.

176 "Well, Mr. President . . . You had it": Interview, January 10, 1969.

178 "You're very much like me": Williams, 322.

178 "I am not ever going to punish . . . had done everything": Williams,
7102.

183 "'Black' is an adjective . . . any reason to change it": Marshall, *His
Speeches*, 503.

184 "The boss wants to see you . . . faith in my husband": See www.
discoverlbj.org/item/oh-marshallt-19690710-1-74-216.

Chapter 11:
A More Perfect Union

187 "The framers of our Constitution . . . in the same Constitution":
Marshall, 201.

188 "He's one of the most . . . aspect of the Constitution, with
remarkable success": Haygood, 20.

188 "a man whose work has symbolized and spearheaded the struggle of
millions of Americans before the law": Haygood, 20.

189 "Is my understanding correct . . . nobody know how it started off":
Haygood, 24.

190 "gentle stirring in seats": Haygood, 26.

191 "Do you subscribe . . . police lineup?": Haygood, 27.

191 "My answer would have to be the same . . . distinction of mind":
Haygood, 29.

192 "Well, Senator . . . give you the answer": Marshall, *His Speeches*, 492.

192 "I want the answer now . . . members of the committee?" *Speeches*,
492.

196 "unwavering commitment to . . . basic principles of civil rights and
civil liberties": Marshall, *His Speeches*, 295.

197 "Thurgood was profoundly affected . . . I could do": Williams,
6992.

197 "it was a rough night": Williams, 7006.

197 "What's shakin,' Chiefy Baby?": Williams, 7610.

198 "Yes, Massah": Crowe, 190.

198 "NOT YET!": Williams, 7158.

199 "I have a lifetime appointment . . . jealous husband": Williams, 7967.

201 "posed for the Courts . . . in actual differences": Marshall, *His
Speeches*, 514.

203 "arbitrary or purposeless . . . intent": *Bell v. Wolfish*, 441 U.S. 520
(1979).

205 "at large": *City of Mobile v. Bolden* 446 U.S. 55 (1980).

206 "Once in a while . . . keeps a lot in:" Williams, 7924.

208 "defective from the start . . . bloody Civil War": Marshall,
His Speeches, 280.

210 "What's going on . . . those Supreme Court judges, right?" Williams,
"Marshall's Law."

211 "My Dear Mr. President . . . Thurgood Marshall": "My Dear
Mr. President," *New York Times*, June 28, 1991. Available here: www

.nytimes.com/1991/06/28/us/l-my-dear-mr-president-601191.html.

211 "What's wrong with me . . . with an opinion": News clip from the
June 28, 1992 press conference available here: www.c-span.org/
video/?c4224184/marshalls-reasons-retireing.

212 "To get along without me": Rosenthal, Andrew. "Marshall Retires
from High Court." *New York Times,* June 28, 1991. Available here:
www.nytimes.com/1991/06/28/us/marshall-retires-from-high-
court-blow-to-liberals.html.

212 "He did what he could with what he had": Page, Clarence. "The
Legacy of Thurgood Marshall," *The Chicago Tribune,* June 30, 1991.
Available here: www.chicagotribune.com/news/ct-xpm-1991-06-30-
9102270600-story.html.

213 "We thank you . . . irrevocably and forever": Williams, 8180.

Chapter 12:
Legacy

214 "We make movies . . . Marshall." Williams, 80.

218 Statistics on diversity in Congress, from www.pewresearch.org/fact-
tank/2019/02/08/for-the-fifth-time-in-a-row-the-new-congress-is-
the-most-racially-and-ethnically-diverse-ever/

218 Statistics on the numbers of minorities in professorships from
"Diversifying the Faculty," Association of American Colleges and
Universities, available here: www.aacu.org/publications-research/
periodicals/diversifying-faculty

219 "Make America great again": See Ronald Reagan in 1980 here:
www.youtube.com/watch?v=FjkX_IBYQHw

219 "rethreaded the Constitution . . . fabric of the nation": Haygood, 4.

Bibliography

Interviews, Videos, Letters

Anderson, Carol, Professor of African American Studies, Emory
University. Interview, available here: www.youtube.com
/watch?v=qeCjvqFKxMo

Brown, DeNeen L. August 18, 2016. "Thurgood Marshall's interracial
love: 'I don't care what people think. I'm marrying you.'" Available
here: www.washingtonpost.com/local/thurgood-marshalls
-interracial-love-i-dont-care-what-people-think-im-marrying
-you/2016/08/18/84f636be-54d5-11e6-bbf5-957ad17b4385_story
.html?utm_term=.ec28a3c72c47

Jefferson, Thomas to William Johnson, June 12, 1823, available here:
founders.archives.gov/documents/Jefferson/98-01-02-3562

Kennedy, John F. June 11, 1963, speech addressing the nation after the racial
turmoil in Alabama, available here: www.nbcnews.com/id/52176687/t/
watch-jfks-civil-rights-speech-years-ago/#.XEDdVy2ZNpI

Marshall, Cissy Suyat. Interview, Library of Congress,
available here: www.loc.gov/resource/afc2010039
.afc2010039_crhp0097_Marshall_transcript/?st=gallery

Marshall, Thurgood. Interview with Mike Wallace, Tuesday, April 16, 1957,
available on YouTube, www.youtube.com/watch?v=IoPLitU6jVg

———. Speech at the Congressional Black Caucus awards, September 14,
1988. Available on YouTube: www.c-span.org/video/?4519-1
/tribute-justice-thurgood-marshall

———. Interview, July 10, 1969. Available here: www.discoverlbj.org/item
/oh-marshallt-19690710-1-74-216

Reagan, Ronald. Speech at the 1980 convention. www.youtube.com
/watch?v=FjkX_IBYQHw

Bibliography

Books

Chemerinsky, Erwin. *Constitutional Law: Principles and Policies*. New York, NY: Aspen Publishers, 2006.

Crowe, Chris. *Thurgood Marshall (Up Close)*. New York, NY: Viking, 2008.

Gibson, Larry. *Young Thurgood: The Making of a Supreme Court Justice*. New York, NY: Prometheus Books, 2012.

Haygood, Wil. *Showdown: Thurgood Marshall and the Supreme Court Nomination that Changed America*. New York, NY: Alfred A. Knopf, 2015.

Kluger, Richard. *Simple Justice: The History of* Brown v. Board of Education *and Black America's Struggle for Equality*. New York, NY: Vintage, 1975.

Marshall, Thurgood. *His Speeches, Writings, Arguments, Opinions, and Reminiscences*. Edited by Mark V. Thushnet. Chicago, IL: Lawrence Hill Books, 2001.

———. *Supreme Justice: Speeches and Writings*, ed. by J. Clay Smith Jr. Philadelphia, PA: University of Pennsylania Press, 2003.

Rosen, Jeffrey. *The Supreme Court: The Personalities and Rivalries that Defined America*. New York, NY: Henry Holt, 2007.

Sunstein, Cass R. *#Republic: Divided Democracy in the Age of Social Media*. Princeton, NJ: Princeton University Press, 2008.

Articles

Apprey, Cheryl Burgan et al., *Peer Review*, summer 2010. "Diversifying the Faculty," Association of American Colleges and Universities, available here: www.aacu.org/publications-research/periodicals/diversifying-faculty.

Bialik, Kristen, "For the Fifth Time in a Row, the New Congress Is the Most Racially and Ethnically Diverse Ever," FactTank, Pew Research Center, February 8, 2019, available here: www

Bibliography

.pewresearch.org/fact-tank/2019/02/08/for-the-fifth-time-in-a
-row-the-new-congress-is-the-most-racially-and-ethnically
-diverse-ever.

"Donald Gains Murray Sr. Dies at 72," *The Baltimore Sun*, Thursday,
April 10, 1986. msa.maryland.gov/megafile/msa/speccol/sc2200
/sc2221/000011/000011/pdf/d007116a.pdf.

Fiss, Owen. "Legacy of Thurgood Marshall." 105 *Harvard Law Review* 49
(1991).

"My Dear Mr. President," *The New York Times*, June 28, 1991.
Available here: www.nytimes.com/1991/06/28/us/l-my-dear-mr
-president-601191.html.

"My Next Guest Needs No Introduction," as reported by *USA Today*,
January 12, 2018. www.usatoday.com/story/news/politics
/onpolitics/2018/01/12/obama-weighs/1027893001.

Page, Clarence. "The Legacy of Thurgood Marshall," *The Chicago
Tribune*, June 30, 1991. Available here: www.chicagotribune.com
/news/ct-xpm-1991-06-30-9102270600-story.html.

"Race Intermixture Is Discussed Without Vote," *The Harvard
Crimson*, March 16, 1928. Available here: www.thecrimson.com.
/article/1928/3/16/race-intermixture-is-discussed-without-vote.

Ripple, Kenneth F. "Thurgood Marshall and the Forgotten Legacy of
Brown v. Board of Education." 55 *Notre Dame* L. 471 (1979–1980).
Available here: scholarship.law.nd.edu/law_faculty_scholarship/916.

Rosenthal, Andrew. "Marshall Retires from High Court." *New York
Times,* June 28, 1991. Available here: www.nytimes.com/1991/06/28
/us/marshall-retires-from-high-court-blow-to-liberals.html.

Smith, Gerald L. "A Black Educator in the Segregated South: Kentucky's
Rufus B. Atwood." University Press of Kentucky. (For the years that
Houston was at the NAACP, see page 200.)

"Thurgood Marshall and the West Texas NAACP Connection," *West*

Texas Tribune, July 1, 2009. Available here: westtexastribune.com
/thurgood-marshall-and-the-texas-naacp-connection-p759-1.htm.

Williams, Juan. "Marshall's Law." *Washington Post,* January 7, 1990.
Available here: www.washingtonpost.com/archive/
lifestyle/magazine/1990/01/07/marshalls-law/
eea56d1a-2dd6-48e3-b6de-2493e66d25d2.

———. *Thurgood Marshall: American Revolutionary.* New York, NY:
Random House, 1998.

"The Woman's Rights Convention—The Last Act of the Drama," *N.Y.
Herald*, September 12, 1852, as quoted by Ruth Bader Ginsburg,
"Gender and the Constitution," *U. Cin. L. Rev.* 44 (1975): 1, 3.

Cases Cited

Bell v. Wolfish, 441 U.S. 520 (1979)

Brown v. Board of Education, 347 U.S. 483 (1954)

Buck v. Bell, 274 U.S. 200 (1927)

Chambers v. Florida, 309 U.S. 227 (1940)

City of Mobile v. Bolden, 446 U.S. 55 (1980)

Hale v. Kentucky, 303 U.S. 613 (1938)

Kimble v. Marvel Enterprises, 576 U.S.___ (2015)

Lyons v. Oklahoma, 322 U.S. 596 (1944)

Mempa v. Rhay, 389 U.S. 128 (1967)

Miranda v. Arizona, 384 U.S. 436 (1966)

Missouri ex rel. Gaines v. Canada, 305 U.S. 337 (1938)

Morgan v. Virginia, 328 U.S. 373 (1946)

Murray v. Pearson, 168 Md. 478 (1936)

Plessy v. Ferguson, 163 U.S. 537 (1896)

Reed v. Reed, 404 U.S. 71 (1971)

Sweatt v. Painter, 339 U.S. 629 (1950)

University v. Murray, 182 A. 590 (Md. 1936)

Acknowledgments

Thanks as always to the dedicated and talented team at Abrams: Howard Reeves, Amy Vreeland, Sara Corbett, Steph Stilwell, Sara Sproull, and Kathy Lovisolo. Thanks also to my trusted readers Carole Greeley, Karen Lamming, and Dawn Torrey.

Index

Note: Page numbers in *italics* refer to illustrations.

Index